The contradiction within the soul of humanity

Ernest Dyer

This essay is based on a combination of the introduction and conclusion of my more extensive consideration of warfare in the book: 'Warfare in human history: an evolutionary perspective' (Dyer, 2023)

Published by New Generation Publishing in 2023

First Edition

ISBN: 978-1-80369-737-6

www.newgeneration-publishing.com

New Generation Publishing

Part I

'If civilization is to survive, the expansion of understanding is a prime necessity.'

A.N.Whitehead 'Modes of Thought' (1938, p63)

As the world's people drift relentlessly towards our own destruction we might ask.... is this end for our species the inevitable outcome of evolved human nature expressed and influenced by about 150,000 years of social become civil life? Or can the world's international institutions and nation-state relationships be re-imagined in the image of the possible, in ways that can resolve the many conflictual issues currently confronting us?

These are the existential questions whose brooding presence are central to defining the future of humanity.

We are each born into a world within a set of circumstances usually including a nexus of familial and social relationships. For most this includes at least one active parent and some close and perhaps some extended family, beyond these to childhood friends and neighbours. As we grow, links of varying emotional strengths are made with teachers, work colleagues, adult friends, and more intimate partners. Across these thread a complex mesh of more instrumental interactions with numerous unnamed others whose lives interact with our own, mostly but briefly.

In spatial terms we are aware of a home, a locality, perhaps a village, town, or city, and these within a region, a country; as we grow we gain a wider sense of an awareness of being in a global world. Then later we might learn about our world being but a planet within a solar system, and this drifting languidly within one of the billions of galaxies spread across an immense and seemingly eternal universe. An expansive spatiality that we now assume was initially created at some point of singularity approx 13.8 billion years ago with a predicted life projecting into the future for billions more. Within this profound conjunction of space/time immensity, our own life-times of 70 odd years (if fortunate) seem to be but a brief flicker of consciousness, of singular irrelevance. What can my own existence

1

mean within such awesome dimensions?

My own tiny 'window' of consciousness, during which I can contemplate the Reality within which my life unfolds, is of fundamental relevance to me. Is this time of my being alive but a mysteriously random 'gift', or for too many a life of generally relentless travail or even intense suffering? Is this time offered to bear witness as our history continues to unfold? Have I emerged into an exercise involving some metaphysical absurdity – the absurdity of a purposeless existence within a wider existential context for which I am merely irrelevant? Why am I being taunted by life's absurdity? As bare questions these are unanswerable, but as irrepressible stimulants to thinking they can prompt me to reflect beyond the social relativities and more philosophical conundrums that I have been born into.

I feel that I have in a sense 'found myself' in existence. As an initial encounter this was an existence of my growing up in a comfortable family setting within a proudly working-class community in post WWII South-East London. Up until my teenage years I took the values and guidelines for acceptable behaviour experienced during this time pretty much for granted as being 'normal'. I was socialized into a normality of post-war 'Britishness'. I was enculturalized within a mass of people mostly offering a bovine-like acceptance of class-based division and social circumstances of marked inequalities of wealth and of opportunity.

At about the age of 15 I began to realize two 'facts': God was a fictional construct and that my own life will end – that the world turns without any god beyond the imaginations of believers and will in due course turn without me. Absorbing the implications rather than living as if denying these facts is the challenge that each one of us faces. Many people chose to adopt a perspective that accepts their death, but they then invoke the idea of a god to offer the hope of some form of life beyond their mortality. To assume a truth in some more formal religious structure that allows a level of cognitive resolution to the emotionally disturbing idea of personal death.

The founding 'fathers' of religions set out certain practises required by believers for them to gain access to a life beyond death. Throughout civil life these have included various forms of supplication, a commitment based on faith-related ideas proposed by men (if these claim to mediate a god's commands – collected in various holy texts), and for some of them: animal or human sacrifice, self-flagellation, child abuse both physical (medically unnecessary male circumcision, female genital mutilation[1]) and psychological, as

---

[1] And for some females the experience of even more barbaric forms of circumcision

when a child is saturated in a single religion throughout childhood, so attempting to deny a child the freedom to consider all religious and non-religious metaphysical perspectives. And for a belief in miraculous occurrences usually happening in a distant past and not authentically repeated since, set in circumstances that deny the laws of nature as we have come to know them.

My own socialization was but one form of the many possible social contexts within which children gain early experience of the world. Seeping steadily into my consciousness as I grew towards adulthood was the realization that many people living elsewhere in the world were suffering at the hands of others, or due to political and economic circumstances created by others.

I could daily: on T.V., the radio, in newspapers and in recent years the internet, learn of evil being expressed all across the world and yet the all-knowing, all-powerful, all-good, god that I had been taught to believe cared deeply for 'his' followers was silent. An enigmatic shadowy figure that has from the earliest historical times been cast across much of the civilized world, taking various now codified forms as its assumed presence has mesmerised the faithful. The followers of this or that religion who so often believe that they – whether Christian, Jew, Moslem, Hindu, Buddhist, whatever - have had the amazing good fortune to have been born and socialised into knowledge of the one 'true' religion. And have not simply been the victims of a form of intellectual and emotional abuse inflicted upon them by their parents and a local community. If the leaders of the world religions were to be sufficiently confident in their god's authenticity then why do they determinedly refuse to allow children to grow up free from the relentlessly constraining propaganda of just one religion, and not allow them to experience a wide range of metaphysical beliefs (including agnosticism and atheism)? And so for them to be 'drawn to' a belief rather than, in effect, have one imposed on them by the arbitrary circumstances of birth and the insidiously powerful influence of socialization?

If faith is so strong, why I wonder have so many 20th and 21st century leaders of religions - the Popes, Bishops, Rabbis, Mullahs, Imams, Patriarchs, Ayatollahs, Swamis, Shamans, and various other types of 'cleric' - who have often gained high social status and comfortable material lives from their religious roles - when coming to their natural end, allow the determined deployment of expensive medical technology as they so embarrassingly cling tenaciously to life. When we might expect that they would embrace their passing

---

than practiced on male babies, such as the practice of sewing up a woman's labia majora to leave an opening just wide enough to urinate through but making penetrative sex impossible.

with open arms and bright eyes willingly looking beyond the earthly travails as they accept their 'god-given' natural mortality and pass into the form of heavenly terrain (for some peopled with accommodating virgins for others a land flowing with milk and honey....) that they have reassured so many others would be the glorious fate awaiting a true believer.

Would so many young men have marched to war without some expectation of the afterlife that they had from early childhood been assured would be their fate if they were killed? A supposed afterlife it seems that so many religious leaders try to avoid for as long as possible. Would so many have throughout history accepted gross economic and social inequality if they were not socialized to accepting these conditions as the will of some or other god?

As a teenager I would sometime gaze out to sea or across some heath- or down- land focused on the why of my existence.... why am I here and why am I here at this time and not before or in a time to come: Why did I not experience existence huddled in some prehistoric cave, or seated in some Greek forum listening to Socrates, or in the shelter of a Bodhi tree absorbing the wisdom of Siddhartha Gautama, or hearing the swish of the whip as I crouch over the oars in a Roman galley, toiling in some medieval field, herding goats in the Gobi Desert in the tenth century or making porcelain in some Chinese pottery at about the same time, crossing the Atlantic on the 'middle passage' as a prisoner wrenched from my west African tribal homeland soon to be sold as a slave in some West India market-place to face a future of relentless toil, or picking oakum in some nineteenth-century English work-house or, or, or.... the millions of other circumstances in which young men have found themselves since civil life began. Why now? Why here? Why not at some other time and place did I experience the unique conjunction of individual awareness cast loose within a lived experience of the world rather than the one that I felt was laid-out before me.

When a child why was I merely due to an accident of birth-place able to live in relative comfort, whereas millions of other children were being denied even the basic requirements for reasonable lives. Yes, obviously historical circumstances have provided the relatively comfortable economic conditions for 20th/21st century Britain. Even if these were to some extent the outcome of the exploitation of peoples living within the British Empire and countries where British political and economic hegemony produced conditions of asymmetric power in trade. Famously so with the African slave trade and with China in the nineteenth-century Opium Wars.

But these are post-birth considerations whereas my focus here is on the randomness of when and where we were actually born; the

4

time and place that we 'find ourselves' in life. The writer Blaize Pascal highlighted the uniqueness of being human and alive with his asking: '....there is no reason why here rather than there, why now rather than then......The eternal silence of these infinite spaces frightens me.'

I feel more in awe than frightened at this uniqueness and its possible implications. Just thinking about the earthly why 'here' rather than 'there' leads me to reflect on my own safe, secure, upbringing within a supportive South-London working class community, compared to those born into poverty, economic exploitation, or within a zone of military conflict; communities in turmoil, and in otherwise unsafe locations.

I suspect that all of us have at times in our lives 'glimpsed' aspects of a path towards a different alignment between the world and the lives within which we have found ourselves; Towards the end of this essay I seek only to elaborate on this. This reflective exercise would not involve a personal journey from a-to-b, in the sense of seeking to take the reader from some assumed state of ignorance towards some ultimate state of enlightenment. It is instead a form of journeying designed to stimulate a self-reflective transformation of one's approach to life. Hopefully, as a process of self-affirmation wedded to the commitment to a possible future for humankind more generally. A future we have all surely glimpsed if but in a dream, now understood as a necessary condition for the survival of future generations if they are to avoid a future involving slavery to depersonalized identities that seems to be facing us – with the relentless advance of the stilted being of consumerism, of but instrumental relationships, and a pattern of continuously recursive self-reference; and that's only if we can avoid a thermo-nuclear holocaust and the impending environmental catastrophe facing the world.

As a more empirical framework to my endeavouring to understand evil I am going to posit two key 'facts' about the Reality within which we all live; within which all of our life-journeys - lived reflectively or unreflectively - unfold. The first is that a process we know as evolution has led to humankind becoming aware of its presence on Earth (and increasingly during the last 3000 years, as a presence in a Universe), the product of reflective self-consciousness attuned to learning as a bio-cultural adaptation. This evolutionary process can be understood as being essentially the development of levels (or modes) of consciousness; of biological processes that gave rise to organisms able to process evermore 'information'. And here we have the second 'key fact' – since life on Earth began the sum total of information available (especially as more formal knowledge) to be accessed by consciousness has increased significantly, and the rate of its accumulation is now exponential.

The outcome of the complex interrelationship between rising levels of consciousness and increasing amounts of information has been the progressive widening of the Reality within which we humans live – Reality being that aspect of Being that we can possibly access. We live within what can be termed an 'ecology of information' – a situation at least partially expressed in the vast store of texts that have been passed down to us and in the huge data-bases now available; with programmers able to design algorithms that can nimbly identify significant patterns and processes within this vast store.

The question of why evil, touched on earlier, presumes the presence of human beings and this in turn invites the underlying question of what it means to be human. In order to gain some understanding of the human condition – this strange entity we know in some reflective consideration of ourselves, of what we observe in others, and of what we have learnt about our ancestors – it would be useful to consider the human in the context of its evolution. Biology is the study of life and, as the renowned geneticist Theodosius Dobzhansky suggested, everything in biology makes sense in terms of evolution. If this is perhaps an over-confident generalization the sciences, especially those of geology, zoology, palaeontology and genetics, have provided an accumulating body of knowledge offering convincing evidential substance to the initial work of those such as Gregor Mendel, Charles Darwin, and Alfred Russell Wallace. Allowing some confidence in a meta-theory suggesting that human life has evolved from an initial conjunction of molecular complexity and environmental conditions that pertained on Earth about 3.8 billion years ago.

And, as a result of the characteristics of organic molecules developing, initially via energetic self-replicating molecular change (liable to tiny replication errors) become more clearly genetic transmission, along with changing environmental conditions, have generated the appearance of a wide range of types of organic life-forms. Forms, as both plant and animal life, that have spread throughout the world's oceans and across its landmasses. I will be considering the biomechanisms providing the dynamic for the evolutionary process in more detail in the concluding section of this extended essay, but here I just want to highlight an aspect of evolution that relates to my own perspective on an implication of evolution as this links to the human condition and so to the question of why evil.

As already noted (Dyer, 2021), I want to suggest that the primary direction of evolution – its most creative aspect – has been the appearance of life-forms able to process ever-increasing amounts of information. And this 'amounts' is in terms of both quantitative and qualitative information, so in detail and in complexity. My own understanding of information is that it provides the fabric of the Reality within which all life exists – a non-material (non-baryonic) substance that pervades the whole Universe. Information can be understood as that which arises from the resolution of uncertainty in experience – but I would suggest that the uncertainty here is just the level of 'difference'. Where there is difference within some stimuli there is information. Most obviously with differences such as the arithmetical 1,2,3, or the coding language of computing 0100111, or with an atom of carbon losing an electron to a neighbouring atom of oxygen a 'difference' takes place. Our DNA contains masses of information as does an image of a flag, a tree, or the 'dance' of a bumblebee identifying the location of a food source. If you can imagine nothingness then the stuff of information would be its very opposite in terms of semantic content.

Similar to energy, mass, and space-time, information is another primary entity involved in the fundamental expression of the Universe – information is best understood as having energy but no mass (similar to photons), its energy being observed in action because its energy is context-dependent. What is ostensibly the same information can energize different reactions in different situations. (see Appendix 1 below for more detail on information)

Enigmatically, information is not necessarily out there waiting to be discovered as life-forms develop into new species. A useful perspective can be gained from viewing information as being both out there waiting to be discovered and also as being created as new knowledge accumulates – Reality, as we can know it, is an outcome of the interweaving of both discovery and creativity. At the start of this last sentence I noted 'useful' – a word that gets to the very nub of this text. I eschew any idea of some ultimate truths about the world – science at its best allows some level of confidence in how it describes and explains our experience and the best of philosophy can offer guidance in relation to personal morality and ethics more generally; as to a limited extent can religion (the limitation here being the veracity of the claimed source of wisdom). But truths, however informed (if this 'informed' can be critically important), are human constructions and as such can only be provisional, being based on knowledge available at any time. In recognition of the ontological conditionality of truths I more often use the term 'useful', which implies a sense of purpose. My own purpose, as noted above, being to gain some understanding of the human condition primarily as this relates to the expression of evil in humankind's history. I will translate useful into heuristic devices, and other linguistic tools, designed to provide the conceptual implements posited to enable understanding; so truths framed as being more instrumental conditions used to support the validity of my extended outline.

The conceptual implements, identified as 'modes' of evolutionary developmental stages, that I use to describe my own focus on developing consciousness, as the condition for information processing, are quite crude – those such as: instinct, sentience, consciousness, awareness, self-consciousness, world consciousness. The boundary (as this relates to information processing capacity) between each of these is vague, and more about how behaviours are subjectively defined than anything more precise. The neuro-philosophers Patricia and Paul Churchland (1986 – and more recently Edouard Machery 2008) are particularly critical about the use of what they term traditional 'folk language' to describe states of thinking and the description of mental states. Their views, noted as a form of 'eliminative materialism', include the suggestion that '.....future scientific developments will show that the way we think and talk about the mind is fundamentally flawed.' They argue the need to focus on observable brain processes, and they advocate a more informed set of descriptive/explanatory discriminations, to move beyond the: '....primitive psychological taxonomy of current ordinary language, to some more penetrating and extraordinarily more fertile taxonomy of states drawn from that more advanced neuro-functional account of our brain activity.'

For my own central purpose I do feel that the use of 'folk' concepts, such as sentience, awareness, and self-consciousness, even given their conceptual fuzziness, would be sufficient to understand the theory outlined. The fuzziness only really becomes apparent at the boundaries between my information processing modes and their associated behaviours, which are:

- Response - instinctual/or closely pre-programmed behaviours – e.g. bacteria, plants, sponges
- Sentience as guiding more mobile activity - moving around an environment seeking food or favourable conditions – e.g. beetles, flies, as well as starfish, and primitive fish.
- Awareness - a more developed mode of mobile activity – where behaviour patterns become more complex – e.g. higher fish, lizards, amphibians.
- A level of conscious awareness with more developed sentience but continuing to be focused on quite local habitats (accepting migration) e.g. grazing and hunting terrestrial animals such as

cattle, jaguars, rats, hyenas, bears - as well as birds.
- A more developed form of consciousness observed in a wide range of behaviours where some elements of planning and interactive social activities, up to more complex forms of vocal and physical communication, are exhibited e.g. whales, other cetaceans, and some early evolved primates such as lemurs, loris and tarsiers.
- Self-consciousness – present at a more basic level in chimpanzees, gorillas, orang-utan, baboon, and bonobos, but most obviously in Homo sapiens and some extinct species of the genus Homo, including: habilis, rudolfernsis, floresiensis, neaderthalensis, denisovans, and erectus.

This last mode of self-consciousness as it developed, in behavioural terms, with its most advanced species (Homo sapiens) has been the conduit by which evil has primarily found expression in the world, and my purpose is to endeavour to identify aspects of self-consciousness that have led to this. Another, more quantitative, way of illustrating this evolutionary progression would be based on the fairly valid assumption that consciousness is more developed in animals with 'bigger brains' (in terms of neuron numbers and network complexity). I am not considering consciousness within any species, only identifying a reasonable 'marker' of how the consciousness exhibited by sentient beings has evolved. So, with this reservation see list below starting with organisms evolving from the time known as the Cambrian Explosion (from about 550 m.y.b.p.) when life began to become more complex:

- Roundworm	– 302 neurons	550 m.y.b.p.
- Cockroach	– 1,000,000	320 m.y.b.p.
- Frog	– 16,000,000	200 m.y.b.p.
- Racoon	– 2,149,000,000	135 m.y.b.p.
- Brown Bear	– 9,586,000,000	30 m.y.b.p.
- Fin Whale	– 15,000,000,000	25 m.y.b.p.
- Chimpanzee	– 28,000,000,000	18 m.y.b.p.
- Homo sapien	– 86,000,000,000	150,000 y.b.p. (modern form from about 50,000 y.b.p)

Although quite crude as a measure, the order of this list does, if roughly, correlate neuron numbers with the time of the appearance of these life-forms. Of more relevance is the information-processing capacity of each type of life-form and this can be assessed by the study of the complexity (range) of an animal's behaviour.

Accepting reservations in relation to the relevance of neural interconnectedness and whole body involvement in consciousness, I suggest that if it were possible to identify the sequential line of species leading from the Last Universal Common Ancestor (LUCA - of about 3.8 b.y.b.p., possibly even earlier) of all cellular life to modern Homo sapiens and the relationship between neuron numbers and time of species appearance, then the progressive nature of evolution (in terms of information processing power) would become quite obvious. Neuronal numbers and their patterns of interconnectedness is a robust indicator of information processing capacity and we can see that this capacity has evolved in stages (modes) over time.

This list above takes us to the human mode of 'self-consciousness' but I also want to posit another biological stage of information processing, that which I would very loosely term 'world-consciousness'. A mode where, if human life is to continue, then certain behaviours, linked to novel ways of processing information, will be necessary. Each information-processing mode incorporates behaviour patterns of the prior mode and will have species at the upper end of its mode's information-processing capacity that show elements of the next higher mode.

Even given the relative imprecision of these modes, and the generality of the examples I have included to allow some idea of the information processing capacity relevant for each, I think the reader should be able to see that there has been a steady development in the information-processing capacity of life-forms on earth. And that it is possible to loosely identify various stages (I note as modes) along the way. In themselves the stages are less relevant than the proposition that information-processing has been the dynamic for evolutionary development itself; which is of fundamental importance.

If biological evolution has been (and continues to be) the appearance of species so adapted to be able to process ever more information, then obviously the modern form of the species Homo sapiens is in the vanguard of this development. An anatomically modern form of which appeared about 50,000 y.b.p., initially living in small-groups (bands) sustained by hunter-forager-gatherer types of lifestyle and progressively developing into what is termed civilization, with the social and economic practices and institutions necessary to support this. Nearly four billion years to progress from some relatively simple self-replicating molecules perhaps forming in some alkaline hydrothermal vents deep within the sea to the phenomenon that is twentieth-first century civilization.

It is the mode of consciousness I note as 'self-consciousness' that has given rise to civil life and with it the most awful expression of evil.

As I grew up I became uneasily aware of the evil that has pervaded (indeed at times actually characterised) humankind's history from the earliest time of civil life. Yes, no doubt there was inter-group conflict prior to the development of towns and cities, but it was civil life and associated technologies that elevated localised conflict into wide-ranging warfare.

What do I mean by evil? A working definition would be 'any act that causes unnecessary harm to a human-being'. So the types of harms that could have been avoided if different conditions had pertained; importantly including decisions being made that contributed to forming the conditions. I feel that I should add harm to any animal or other aspects of the living environment but do not want to get distracted, so my focus is on humanity. I want to suggest that we should view evil as acts, not as some essence residing within individuals - a key consideration. This perspective would not absolve individuals for their part in an evil act, but it does prompt the consideration of a wider context involving the social conditions in which the expression of evil is more rather than less likely to occur. And in this sense, offers the grounds for understanding in relation to causation beyond this or that individual or group and so offering the grounds for a more realistic strategy for its possible alleviation.

Let's not get entangled in some over-abstracted philosophical debate, on the meaning of unnecessary, or what constitutes harm. I mean an act that causes harm when there is a clear alternative course of action (including inaction). Just think about any act that could cause harm for or your family that 'could have been avoided' whether this is a drunken motorist, a polluted atmosphere, or a thermonuclear explosion, all realistic threats in today's world. But 'could have been avoided' would also apply to famines, and the various types of natural disasters to which some people – usually the poor - are more vulnerable than others.

Identifying the conditions of could have been avoided for each particular expression of evil is a profound challenge to humanity. The question of could have been avoided links to the political and economic conditions that set the circumstances within which significant harms are liable to take place. Consequently, would it be possible to reform the current national and international economic and political systems, so that these are designed to eliminate the worst expression of evil – the massacres, ethnic cleansing, mass rape, gross economic exploitation, all forms of modern-day slavery, the 5/6 million displaced people living in refugee camps, the millions of children living in poverty, the homeless children endeavouring to survive on the street, the thousands dying in famines due more about access to markets rather than food shortages .... etc. etc. I want to leave this matter for the final chapter of this essay.

I suggest four obvious sources of evil in today's world, each of which threatens the future of humankind:

- Environmental degradation
- Artificial Intelligence - who controls it and its potentially dramatic implications.
- Gross economic inequality – especially in relation to poverty
- Conflict – various forms of warfare.

Whilst these are interrelated, I will be primarily focusing on 'warfare', not least due to my view that if we can tentatively begin to design international conditions conducive for ending warfare and reducing all forms of intergroup conflict to a minimum, then the political and economic conditions necessary for this will impact positively on our ability to focus on alleviating the other three threats.

In order to consider warfare, I will need to go to a dark place. One encapsulated in the very concept of 'war' – the basis of harms between and within nation-states. By my own broad definition the latter would also include within nation ethnic cleansing, which can hardly be termed civil war in the conventional sense as only one side is usually an immediate aggressor, excepting that the one side aggressor can also be an aspect of war involving nation-states when one invades another – The US-led alliance invading Afghanistan (2001) and Iraq in (2003) or the Iraq invasion of Iran (1980-88) and Kuwait (1990), or the Russian invasion of Afghanistan (1979-89) and Ukraine (2022) – just to note some more recent examples – if historically, few countries have not invaded another (usually a neighbouring) country.

PART II

Any consideration of humankind's civil history suggests a strong tendency to resort to violence to achieve what are primarily elite group determined ends. In terms of international politics, these ends have been articulated over the past four centuries in progressing or defending some notional entity termed 'national interest'. Conflict more generally, has been a defining characteristic of civil life when elite-group interests have clashed.

Our past has seen a steaming brew stirring together elements of greed, ambition, ignorance, and power ill-used. The generating conditions for the tracery of evil that has pervaded the human species time on earth.

It is estimated that in the 5,000 years since the beginning of recorded history, from 3,000 BCE onwards, only about 268 years had no recorded warfare, with 14,300 wars having been fought. Just consider the material destruction and human dislocation, death, and general misery caused by this seemingly systemic collective human behaviour.

In the modern period, the twentieth century alone was characterised by destruction − of property, government finance, of lives, and of hopes for humanity's future - in a series of wars interspersed with numerous more localised killing fields as nations - and within nations, ethnically, religiously, or politically divided groups - clashed on the battlefield and also the on the streets of towns and cities. Is there something deep within the nature of humankind that will invariably find expression in violence? Or are we led into conflict due to institutions of governance and the patterns of international relations, and more generally of global political tropes, inherited from the past, made even more terrible by the advancing technology of weaponry? Provisionally we might assume that elements of both could be involved, and so our focus would be on mitigating the influence of our human nature and reconstructing our inherited civil institutions. In our addressing the twin sources creating the pre-conditions for warfare.

The Janus-faced countenance of our species – a moral side prone to co-operation and peaceful coexistence and a more aggressive side prone to competition and conflict – was clearly seen in conditions of international relations in the first half of the twentieth century. The utter futility of WW I with its mud-curdling, blood-curdling, insanity followed by the enlightened setting up of the League of Nations (1920) to arbitrate between nations in dispute. The preamble to its constitution noted that its aims were:

1) To promote international co-operation
2) To secure international peace.

Aspirations reinforced with the signing of the Kellogg-Briand Pact in 1928 (more formally: 'The International Treaty for the Renunciation of War as an Instrument of National Policy'). Initially based on an agreement arranged between Aristide Briand (French P.M) and Frank Kellogg (US Sec. of State) that the two states would agree to renounce war. Given theoretical substance in a multilateral agreement signed by: India, Turkey, Germany, U.K., France, Spain, Soviet Union, USA, China, Norway, Canada, Australia, Japan.....and about 50 other countries.

The authority of the LoN was terminally eroded with its attempts to mediate being in effect ignored on a regular basis throughout the 1920s and 30s, and the noble aspirations of the K-B Pact being ignored by the world's most powerful signatory nations as the world was plunged by them into yet another war engulfing much of its population. At this war's end, many European towns and cities were devastated, Japan had been scorched by visitations of hell, and much of the globe was still being argued over by European nations only being at best grudgingly prepared to accept the post-war surge for independence across much of the ex-colonial territories. At this second global war's end we again see the moral side expressed in the establishment of the United Nations in 1945. The purposes of which was noted in its constitution as:

'The purposes of the Organization should be:
1. To maintain international peace and security; and to that end to take effective collective measures for the prevention and removal of threats to the peace and the suppression of acts of

aggression or other breaches of the peace, and to bring about by peaceful means adjustment or settlement of international disputes which may lead to a breach of the peace;

2. *To develop friendly relations among nations and to take other appropriate measures to strengthen universal peace;*

3. *To achieve international cooperation in the solution of international economic, social and other humanitarian problems; and*

4. *To afford a centre for harmonizing the actions of nations in the achievement of these common ends.'*

Then followed about 100 more wars, including India/Pakistan partition, Korea, Vietnam, Afghanistan, Iraq, Iran, Kosovo, Israel/Palestine from 1948 on......actual wars often involving the world's more militarily powerful nations or what were, in effect, proxy wars fought with their support.

It seems that we have the wish (and the moral intuition) to realise the futility of warfare and the need for international institutions to prevent these, but powerful elements of national leaderships have considered an easy recourse to violence as being a legitimate way to conduct international relations; to progress their perception of their nation's interest.

The costs of war in just human terms (even if omitting the massively destructive impact on built and natural environments) is significant, with the two World Wars of the 20th century alone taking 95 million lives (50 million of these being civilians – WWI 20m dead with 10m of these being civilian, WWII 75m dead with 40m of these being civilians). Since WWII came to an end there has only been 2 days when there has not been open conflict between at least two nations; these being the 2nd and 28th Sept 1945. Since 1945 warfare has added about another 10m casualties in: - Korea, Vietnam, Algeria, and Iraqi invasion of Iran and Kuwait, Russian invasion of Afghanistan and Ukraine, Chinese invasion of Tibet, American invasion of Iraq and Afghanistan, etc. In sum: 200 million plus have died as a result of 20th and early 21st century warfare, over half of these being civilians.

Just consider the economic resources poured and continuing to pour into military preparation and the actual expression of international conflict. Today the global spending on the military is running at $2 Trillion per year (2021), with the three highest spending nations being Russia $62 Billion (2021), China $252 Billion (2021), UK $62 Billion (2021), Saudi Arabia $58 Billion (2021 est.), and the USA $778 Billion (2021); these all on rising trends. A waste of resources on a vast scale each and every year – just consider what could be done with such funding for good rather than as preparation for evil in the world.

What sense can there be in young people from different countries, who have themselves never met, coming together with the intention to kill each other? What sense is there in launching missiles, and dropping bombs on cities, towns, and villages, when experience shows that most of the casualties will be non-combatant civilians, including many children? What sense is there in turning civil infrastructures into rubble, farmland into wasteland, and waterways into toxic flows? All being just the more obvious impact of military conflict.

The consequent question to engaging in such a nonsensical activity would be........Whose interests are being served by fostering such inter-nation conflict? Who benefits from our living in a world where international diplomacy is pervaded which an overwhelming aura of between-nation antagonisms and background conditions of aggressive economic competition and political hegemony? I would like to, just briefly, consider some of the more obvious aspects of this question.

In recent centuries the most obvious interest would the vast fortunes made by arms companies, various types of 'security' companies, and invariably financial speculators. Then there are political leaders endeavouring to deflect opposition to domestic economic and/or political failure. Or due to the more insidiously mundane fact that for our current national leaders an alternative perspective (one based more on the longer-term 'interests' of the whole world's people) does not form an aspect of their mindset. Today's leaders have been politically nurtured to interpret international relations primarily in terms of aggressive economic competition and threatened or actual military conflict. This is their psychological 'comfort zone', one infused by an intentional perspective based on assumptions gained during their socialization within this or that, usually quite privileged (elitist) socio/political context. And these represent just the primary interests served by the conflictual milieu that pervades international relations. A crude but clear set of correlations can be made between the decisions taken by national leaders and the means of furthering the interests of their own elite class and in some countries the even more specific interests of their own family.

I wish to focus on international relations here, but of course within-nation civil wars have been and are also significant expressions of evil. In places such as Yemen, Mali, Afghanistan, Somalia, Myanmar, Tigray, DCR, Libya, and Turkey, communities are currently being torn apart by inter-group violence: groups divided by religion, ethnicity, tribalism, or by political ambitions. I would expect that if we can outline a viable alternative to global governance than that which currently pertains, this would also contribute to providing conditions, including political mechanisms, conducive to at least easing within-nation conflict.

If international relations based on sovereign nation-statehood at least pretend to be suitable for overcoming the primary issues facing the world's people, then recent history alone suggests that this is a seriously flawed assumption. It probably seems obvious, but should we not have aims for world peace, the end of poverty, access to decent healthcare, housing, and education for all being quite minimal aspirations for the world's people. The obviousness stems from the repeated claims made, from at least mid. 20th century, by a series of mendacious politicians in whose speeches these aims have had the substance sucked out to become mere husks containing a residue of but empty promises.

And failure in any one of the four critical issues will impact on significant numbers of the global population:

- Environmental degradation.
- Warfare (military conflict), both conventional military engagement and the possibility of nuclear catastrophe.
- A.I. and its implications
- Significant and increasing economic inequality (of more importance, significant poverty).

This essay has a focus on warfare but each of these critical elements impacting on our species can be considered as interrelated.

An evil activity closely associated with warfare is the act of massacre, sometimes to the point of genocide. And even just the twentieth century saw a series of massacres, a list that began with the Saan, Namaqua, and Herero peoples of West Africa between 1904-08 (about 100,000 killed). Those that followed included: the Armenian massacre of 1915 (1.5m killed); the Nanking atrocities during the second Sino-Japanese war in 1937; the relentless killing (100million) often amounting to massacres...... of service personnel in the sea, air and land battlefields and of civilians in the villages, towns, and cities - especially the Russian military and civilian casualties on the eastern front - the extreme carpet bombing of German and British cities, and equally destructive fire and nuclear bombing of Japan - during the two World Wars; the murderous dictatorships of Stalin,

Suharto, and Mao Zedong, the many 'death-squads' tasked with the elimination of those who have opposed dictatorships such as those of Videla (Argentina), Pinochet (Chile) and Somoza (Nicaragua) in South America, and those bands of state-sponsored murderers in Nazi occupied Europe, and more recently in Africa - and the multiple bloody acts of terrorism throughout the century - the 'holocausts' perpetrated by the regimes led by Hitler/Nazis (6m – Europe 1939-45) and Pol Pot/Khmer Rouge (1m - Cambodia/Kampuchea 1976-79); the communal strife killing over 1 million during the birth of India and Pakistan in 1947; the killing fields of Rwanda with 800,000 people massacred in but 100 days of 1994.

Then there are what were in effect massacres of populations due to indifference, including the millions that died due to famines in Russia, India, China, and Eastern Africa, in a world of sufficient food; the estimated (UNICEF) 1.5 million children who do not reach the age of 5 annually due to vaccine preventable diseases (over 4,000 per day), with another 1200 dying each day of malaria and 2 million children dying each year of diseases contracted due to contaminated water.........and the too many similar macro expressions of avoidable evil together representing the very bleakest aspect of humanity. A systemic evil with effective foundations in global economic and political arrangements.

In part, a sense of collective amnesia perhaps induced by disaster overload – we are (or choose to be) but impotent witnesses as history unfolds in shapes determined by the more powerful in ways strongly influenced by the past. We, being more passively entertained than actively informed by brief if repeated exposure to vivid media imagery and conventionally impotent interpretations. Interpretations that only make sense within the artfully constructed frameworks of our own social relativities.

Milan Kundera tellingly notes how news of each new atrocity obscures the preceding one '.......as so on and so forth until ultimately everyone lets everything be forgotten.'[2]

The generalized socialization processes to which we are subject, including any society's normalized value system, not only influences how we view events but also offer some assumed context for how these events are presented to us by political and economic interests and by the media; the power-bases of modern society. When individuals, whether they be Hitler, Stalin, Pol Pot, or Suharto, or

---

[2] Cited in J.Glover, 2001, p4 – the original being Kundera's 'The Book of Laughter and Forgetting', 1982

more recently Saddam Hussein, Radovan Karadžić, Bashar al-Assad, and Vladimir Putin, are in fact but elements of the – historical, social, economic, political - conditions in which any evil is expressed. Psychotic individuals might well play a key role in an evil action, but it is systemic dysfunction in governance that allows them to rise to positions of power.

In evil acts such as the carpet bombing of the German city of Dresden or the fire-bombing of the Japanese city of Tokyo in 1945 or the spraying of the toxic defoliant Agent Orange over farmlands and villages in Vietnam in the late 60s and early 70s, most 'westerners' would be reluctant to classify Britain's then Prime Minister Winston Churchill, or the then US Presidents Franklin D. Roosevelt, Lyndon B. Johnson and Richard Nixon, as psychopaths.

And yet the outcomes of their decision-making – the killing of thousands of non-combatant, men, women, children, babies - were surely pure evils.

Eric Hobsbawm noted that in relation to the 20th century: '...more human beings had been killed or allowed to die by human decision than ever before in history.' He references an estimate of 187 million killed up to 1993 made by Z. Brezezinski (Brezezinski 1993, cited in Hobsbawn, 1995, p12).

Twentieth-century conflicts have more often involved neighbouring countries. With obvious current between-nation disputes being: India/Pakistan - China/Japan - China/USA – NATO/Russia – Russia/Ukraine - Palestine/Israel – Serbia/Kosovo - China/Taiwan - Venezuela/Honduras – Armenia/Azerbaijan - USA/Iran. And in addition, a range of civil wars, with the more significant being; Libya, Yemen, Turkey (Kurds), Mali, Burkina Faso, Niger, Mozambique, Syria, Somalia, Ethiopia. These too many situations with the potential for minor, border or other, clashes to escalate into more significant, even possibly nuclear, confrontation. In any conflict between antagonists heavily invested in complex computer-based technology there is also the potential for error.

Even during periods of the hegemonic normality of international relations the danger of escalation is an ever-present possibility - As recently as June 2021 HMS Defender, a British warship was on passage through the Black Sea, off Cape Fiolent on the Crimean coast, in what the UK considers to be international waters but Russia views as being within its own territorial waters. A Russian coastguard vessel moved to intercept the warship and a number of Russian S24 jet aircraft flew low over the ship. There were different claims, not just on the legitimacy of the passage, but also on the context of the confrontation. But whoever ordered HMS Defender to take the route it did (and conveniently took the highly unusual step of inviting a number of journalists to join the voyage) was well aware of the potential for confrontation. Globally, these sort of what hostile/provocative contacts seem to happen on a fairly regular, pretty much 'tit for tat', basis by countries in dispute over some aspect of their assumed sovereignty.

We might ask why British warships would be exercising in the Black Sea, or why the Russians have increased their own activity in the Arctic Sea. No doubt part of the general provocative activity engaged in by both 'sides'; the military element of hegemonic diplomacy. We might even pose the question..... why 'sides' in a world we share?

And of course – similar types of provocation (brinksmanship) are regularly engaged in by other nations: China and Japan with islands in the south-China Sea, China and Taiwan, India and Pakistan over Kashmir, North Korea with South Korea and Japan, Ukraine and Russia over the Crimean Peninsula and more recently the whole of the Donbas region. With most neighbouring unfriendly states undertaking intentionally provocative sabre-rattling military manoeuvres in their border regions.

For egoistic nation-states, the narrowing politico/military mindset leads to easily making threats and issuing warning that are difficult to draw back from. The current language deployed in international relations is suited to contributing to quite easily transforming an issue into a crisis and on to escalate into open conflict.

Conventional warfare has been truly terrible......wasting lives, spreading misery, degrading environments, and using vast amounts of economic resources that could have been available to do good rather than evil. We now also live within the shadow of thermonuclear warfare and a sense that it could begin imminently, as the many more local conflicts involving nuclear powers progress incrementally and irrationally to the highest level of politico/military tensions.

Such are the weapons now available that the next global conflict could see the elimination of millions of civilians within but a few days of a nuclear exchange and with a global environment unable to support human (or much other) life. And for sure, if we continue with the same malfunctioning – competitive, conflictual, and hegemonic – international system, and do not adopt some form of effective global governance in relation to international conflict, it is highly likely that such an exchange will soon engulf us. Just nine of the world's 210 countries together hold a sufficiency of nuclear weapons to render our planet uninhabitable for human life.

As of 2023 there are a total of about 12,700 nuclear warheads in store or readied for use. These to be carried by bombers parked at military airports, at sea on aircraft carriers, by intercontinental missiles nestled in numerous deeply buried silos sited across the continents, and in nuclear armed submarines on continuous patrol in the silent depths of the world's oceans.

The atomic warhead – 'Little Boy' - used to destroy the Japanese city of Hiroshima in August 1945 had an explosive power equivalent to 15,000 tons of TNT. The US has tested and deployed warheads such as the one named 'Castle Bravo', with an explosive power equivalent to 15 megatons of TNT, so 1,000 times more powerful than the bomb used at Hiroshima. Russia has tested and deployed a warhead named the 'TSAR Bomba' with an explosive power of a staggering 50 megatons, so equivalent to 3,300 times the power of the Hiroshima warhead. 'TSAR Bomba' has a killing zone of 1,000 kilometres from the initial blast and spreading potentially lethal levels of radiation as clouds drift way beyond this. There has over the past 70 odd years been a veritable escalation in a macabre competition between the world's leading nations to find the means of killing as many human beings – men, women, children and babies - as possible. And of course in doing so they are, via the attempt to maintain a balance of mutually assured destructive power (MAD), also increasing the threat to their own peoples.

We have been exposed to images of mushroom-like clouds rising serenely over unseen terrain – from which we can hardly gain any realistic sense of just what the cloud represents in human terms. For Britannica (online – 23/05/2022): 'When a nuclear weapon detonates a fireball occurs with temperatures similar to those at the centre of the Sun.'

Within the first minute of an initial explosion about 85% of the thermonuclear energy is as air pressure blast and thermal radiation energy and about 15% as radiation 'clouds'. The air pressure blast expresses itself as a nuclear fireball that explodes at ground zero and in seconds would expand out to engulf the surrounding land for hundreds of miles around. Almost all life within the immediate killing zone is burnt off the face of the earth within a couple of minutes, but the highly ionised radiation then forms a nuclear wind that will drift way beyond the immediate killing zone, to degrade the environment and inflict often fatal doses of radiation sickness as it spreads. The immediate killing zone for a single thermonuclear device could easily destroy a city the size of those such as: London, New York, Moscow, Islamabad, Mumbai, Buenos Aires, Mexico City, Jakarta, Manila, Tokyo, Jerusalem, Paris, Beijing, Pyongyang, and leave their extensive hinterlands as but radiation wind-blown wastelands.

If just 1% of the currently held nuclear warheads were to be used (so a 'relatively' low-level exchange) the likely desolation impacting beyond the immediate killing zone would lead to 2 billion people dying of starvation as a result of a global famine caused by the ensuing nuclear winter.

A more significant and probably more realistic scenario of conflict between Russia and the US would be the exchange of about 3,000 warheads (Russia has 4,477 warheads readily available and the US has 3,708). The explosive energy released would generate millions of tons of soot rising into the atmosphere, this happening within but 6 minutes, would reduce the amount of sunlight reaching the earth's surface to about 35% of current amounts. Consequently, the earth would enter a nuclear induced winter lasting for decades, during which food production would be cut by about 90%. Within two years 75% of the world's population will be dead and those that remain will be living on an irradiated planet with conditions inducing, still births, deformed babies, and a veritable eruption in the number of cancer cases for decades on.

Of the nine currently nuclear-armed nations, each has an identified 'enemy' to threaten and to be threatened by. All of the global nuclear powers are involved in some level of inter-nation tension that highlights the possible costs in human terms of allowing an issue to escalate into armed conflict and so the potential to progress to a nuclear exchange if one side appears to be 'losing'. And the losing will be judged as such by egocentric leaders who will themselves be safely ensconced deep underground in well-provisioned nuclear shelters when they launch a nuclear Armageddon.

These same leaders who are at least assumed to be tasked to protect the populations they represent currently allow international conditions to pertain that are based on conflictual and competitive relationships rather than on the recognition of mutual interests – their primary interest should surely be the maintenance of peace.

However sophisticated are the measures designed to prevent an accidental launch of these fearsome weapons the risk of human, or more likely technical, error remains. Since 1950 there have been 32 documented accidents involving nuclear weapons (and these only the ones known of in a context of obsessive secrecy – coded as 'national security') – these 'broken arrow' events highlight the risks involved in maintaining such weaponry.

In the 1960s the world was taken to the brink of nuclear war over the Cuban Missile Crisis, an egocentric argument over the siting of Russian missiles on the Caribbean Island of Cuba (the US already had nuclear-armed missiles sited in Turkey, close to the Russian border). – We know that some US generals were arguing for a first strike nuclear launch, I think that we can fairly assume that Russian generals have been doing similar urging of their political leadership, and we can be certain that if one side launched then so would have the other - millions killed, extensive infrastructural damage. Because two nations were engaged in a macabre provocation/reaction diplomatic game the consequences of which could have been far in excess of any rational evaluation of the issue.

As US President Ronald Regan and USSR President Mikhail Gorbachov agreed when they met in 1985 'A nuclear war cannot be won and must never be fought'. And yet the leadership of both nations have continued to prepare for just such an event as each nation continued to build its nuclear strike capability.

In a context of rising military tension, mutual suspicion, inflated egos of the politico/military leadership, a wide range of true and falsified information to be evaluated as well as numerous 'what if' scenarios having to be considered - consequently we have politicians and the heads of armed services being potentially overwhelmed by streams of information and having to balance arguments for action from an aggressive military and counter arguments from more moderate advisors, whilst having to assess streams of often new and usually quite complex information – the emotions could easily come to override any rational decision-making. We can see a reflection of this during the 1960s Cuban missile crisis (noted above) where, if a significant nuclear exchange had occurred as a result of the Russians sitting missiles on the island of Cuba, then potentially hundreds of millions of civilians would have been killed in initial the strikes, with hundreds of millions more dying during subsequent years from burns and radiation poisoning – whereas even if missiles had been sited on Cuba (as the US itself had already sited missiles in Turkey within a few miles of the Russian border) this would not have any significant impact on the defence or attack capability of each superpower. The mutually assured destruction (MAD) balance would have been maintained.

So whilst, if we step back we can accept the sheer irrationality of thermonuclear confrontation, we would, at least in the short-term need to introduce some protection, some 'trip switch' to prevent an immediate decision to launch missiles due to politico/military agents reacting emotionally in the heat of escalating confrontation and of information overload as an event plays out rather than stepping back to take decisions in a calmer setting. And bear in mind that the extensive – global – impact of a thermonuclear exchange would include the possible extinction of humanity and indeed of most other mammalian life on earth.

The necessary 'trip-switch' could be embodied in a form of international governance. Just a no first strike commitment would be something. But even better would be a commitment of the nine nuclear-armed nations to allow the Head of (a reformed) UN to order a suspension of verbal exchanges and of any conflict on the ground that is escalating towards a potentially immediate uplift to the nuclear. This to allow a pause in confrontation and so a chance to recalibrate the response to what has been assessed by each side as aggressive action by the other party. Many of the World's leaders and senior military just do not seem to get what Mutually Assured Destruction actually means.

The threat of nuclear conflict is real, with the major powers still, even post START (began 1980s), bristling with nuclear weaponry in conditions of rumbling international conflicts, each with the potential to conflagrate into warfare. Even relatively lowly nuclear armed Britain has access to some formidable weaponry – it has a nuclear fleet composed of four Trident submarines each armed with 16 missiles, each one of which is eight times as powerful as the weapon dropped on Hiroshima in 1945. With this weaponry alone Britain has the capability to destroy 64 major cities within 7,500 miles of its mobile craft. There is an estimated 10,200 nuclear warheads in the hands of the World's military. That's over 10,000 of the world's cities that can be totally destroyed – with the loss of hundreds of millions of lives in an immediate exchange and no doubt similar numbers subsequently dying from radiation sickness, and many more from the extensive damage that would be done to civic infrastructure and to the world's environment.

More generally, the technology of war-making is progressively involving artificial intelligence – advanced drone technology, robotics, and other computer-based innovation have been primary features if 21st century life. The world's military has sought to both drive this advance and ensure that it can be applied to battlefield weapon systems, intercontinental missile design, and intelligence gathering.

The advance of all forms of artificial intelligence are developing at an accelerating pace, primarily driven by the search for evermore financial profit, by the military itself, and by governments and security companies seeking the means for ever greater observation and control over populations. The potential human benefits are merely used to 'sell' the idea to populations rather than these actually leading the development and control of the technology. Conflict, in its planning, preparation, and engagement, is becoming ever more reliant on types of A.I. So a potential source or real harm to human beings. (see Appendix 2 'Artificial Intelligence: a possible scenario', for more on this)

Any overview of the history of conflict would identified that the most critically obvious feature of conflict is 'difference'. Of one group of people.... be it tribe, clan, class, ethnic group, religion, nation, or federation of these, identifying another similar group as being different and holding to views on an issue that differ from their own. The evolutionary mode of self-consciousness tends towards favouring the world-view and more general descriptive and explanatory tropes of one's own group and rejecting or being suspicious of alternatives expressed by outsiders – the 'others'. There does seem to be a natural propensity to auto-consciously gravitate towards within-group identity. At times the theoretically neutral acceptance of difference can become antagonist and even to escalate into conflict. Throughout civil history ruling elites have known how to manipulate this seemingly natural propensity toward 'othering' via the fostering of suspicion, and the use of propaganda and other forms of persuasion. Underlying any group difference is of course a unity in our shared species identity and if we are to find an alternative to intergroup conflict, not least warfare, we need to design ways to socialise people into transcending the relativity of group identity (more often an accident of time and place of birth).

Nation-statehood (along with religion) is probably the most powerful, and currently for the World the most dangerous, entity fostering the identification of difference between peoples. Difference being the basic originating marker of separation that so easily spreads and erupts into the pathological fault-lines upon which conflict between peoples is founded. States and Nations are different concepts – the concept of state merely represents some form of political sovereignty over a geographic area, whereas the concept of nation usual includes this but in addition we invariably have an archly selective version of history, usually a common language, and all the other social and economic elements that constitute the 'imagined community' noted by Benedict Anderson (1983). You can have nations without statehood as in the pre-Israel Jewish Diaspora, The Kurdish peoples, and certain Moslems sects which believe in a global Ummah where the gravitational pull of Islam draws in some primary characteristics of nationhood traditionally treated as secular.

It might seem to be obvious, but at least one group has to see a difference between themselves and another group for conflict to ensue. And nation-statehood (as well as tribe, caste, class, religion, and ethnicity more generally) is a seemingly automatic marker of difference that we are each born into – and within which we are subjected to the powerful socialization processes that are (implicitly and explicitly) designed to emphasize the good aspects of one's own country and the bad aspects of others. The inherited form that relationships between nation-states have taken is of competition and conflict rather than cooperation and an enlightened acceptance of mutually shared interest. Any between nation-state co-operation has been more about gaining allies for competing with another nation or groupings of these, often including the superficial pretence of some common values.

We have inherited an international political and economic system that assumes conflict and competition, but can we learn to re-set how we live together as nations? Is there an alternative way of organizing international relationships? Or is humanity condemned forever to drag the divisive political and economic institutions created in conditions of greed, aggression, avarice, suspicion, and fear, into the future? When from the earliest time of civil life such conditions being primarily promoted by elite groups and subsequently maintained by their descendants and others who have since joined the elites. If 'forever' might be dramatically foreshortened by human species extinction...... perhaps in some nuclear conflagration or due to making the world's environment progressively unable to sustain a viable human population.....or even a combination of these. The point being that if conflict, tipping into warfare, is based on choices, individual and collective, then there is always the option to choose peace rather than war. We can, at least potentially, find an alternative way to live together. A key element if we aspire to some form of peaceful world governance would be the need to address the role (purpose) of the nation-state.

Nation states in their modern types are a relatively recently established form of political organization (for Jürgen Habermas 1969, p109, 'State and nation have fused into the nation-state only since the revolutions of the late eighteenth century.'), with institutions effectively designed by generations of elite groups. Those who, as a class, have accumulated both hard and soft power to themselves. Institutions designed in their own perceived interests, as aided initially by the printing press and national education systems each contributing to creating and spreading the use of common versions of national languages and assumed national histories. And more recently aided by a xenophobic mass media controlled according to corporate interests, often as guided by billionaire owners who assume the privilege to interpret news and produce info- and enter-tainment in line with their own reactionary political views. Mass populations, from earliest childhood until old age, are now being drenched with information in forms redolent of the competitive, conflictual, mindset that determines international relations. The mendacious construction of external enemies can be used to reinforce control by elite groups over national populations.

Obedience, at times jingoistic enthusiasm, has more often been realised as the default behaviour of the masses, so allowing divisions to be fostered by elite groups able to gain advantage from this fracturing of the potentially unifying resources available for the masses - resources that include the potential to transcend national borders which were after all mostly only created on the basis of fiefdoms of local or regional exploitation.

The world's peoples' have over the last 500 years been progressively and artificially divided ('separated') into nation-states, each with a range of ideas that congeal to create some assumed sense of a 'national interest' which can include the economic (markets and resources), claimed territorial rights, and a self-reflective (too often oversensitive) national ego saturated in selected versions of history.

The early civil history of political organization, circa 3,000 BCE, was characterised by city-states as circumscribed units of centralized power; if with some at times expedient regional confederations of these. As certain cities, or federations, became more powerful (in terms of ambitious leaderships and surplus material resources available to equip and support armies) they sought to expand their control, and more widely their hegemonic influence. This in places developed into empires, some more prominent ones have been: Mesopotamian, Macedonian, Mauryan, Roman, Islamic, Gupta, Han, Inca, Aztec, Mogul, Axum, Benin, British, Ottoman, and Hapsburg. Empires, each constituted by a multiplicity of ethnic groups, with most being run by an elite section of a dominant one of these.

In addition to the contribution of both printing in promoting national languages and the development of national education systems, to the formation of nation-states noted above, the 15th/16th century voyages of 'discovery', and associated mapping of the world, provided a territorial perspective serving to provide graphic representation of potential areas of trading or more directly controlling interests (exploitation). The processes of forming the large volunteer or, from about the 1790s conscripted, military units developed to fight European wars, also contributed to forming national mythologies – with impressive statues and other monuments constructed to remind populations of this archly edited past. These, and some other less obvious processes, created the cloying notion of a national identity which could then generate the idea of some 'national interest' and for providing some assumed justification for an aggressive approach to foreign policy.

Noam Chomsky (2012, p196) noted the 'national interest' as being a form of nation-state international perspective that is something '....abstracted from [the] distribution of domestic power.'

So highlighting how this national interest is created in any country primarily to reflect elite group priorities – those who have domestic power. Be they from: corporations, the mass media, the military, landed aristocracy, political groupings, oligarchs, religious leaders, financiers, speculators and the legions of lobbyists (and Franz Fanon's other types of modern 'bewilderers') who so determinedly represent them.

The European types of nation statehood provided models to be adopted, if more-often only awkwardly adapted to local circumstances, by ruling groups across the world. And, primarily for European elites, nationalism became an artful means of legitimising imperial expansion and exploitative forms of colonialism. It was the European nation states, increasing influenced by powerful merchants and financiers that enthusiastically engaged in a shameless international conflict over land, trading rights, and other resources in the Americas, the Middle and Far East and, by the 18th century, Africa.

European nation-states were created in conditions of military conflict, economic exploitation, and often violent between-nation competition over trading rights and in seeking primary resources. It was these intentional elements that served as core determinants constructing national institutions and shaping the approach taken to foreign policy. The perception of the world as being there for the taking, assuming competition over valued goods in what was assessed as being a zero-sum game, with each nation determined to gain as big a share of the bounty as possible. Seeking to advance its elite constructed notions of national self-interest, at whatever cost in sweat, blood, and lives, to indigenous peoples.

It is the 19th and 20th versions of strategic military, economic, and diplomatic, strategies based on systemically operative notions of national self-interest primarily serving the interests of elite groups that have set the scene for today's international political arrangements. Arrangements, prominent in which are the more powerful 'empires of influence' (China, USA, and Russia, today) – if underlying these there is the dislocated empire of global finance. All of the world's people are now inveigled within a global conspiracy of assumed division.

Up to about 1500 C.E. by far the majority of the world's people, even within empires, had lived their lives within an identity based on the quite local and in accepting the power (control) of some more regional or city-based hierarchy with a variety of types of feudal lord or chieftain at its head. In Europe, it was from this class of lordships and chieftains, along with a wider aristocratic class, that sought to dominate the earliest of states being formed during the almost continuous conflict that characterised medieval Europe. By the end of the sixteenth century much of Europe had been divided into individual 'states' run by elite groups, gaining authority by assumed heredity rights, by the power of arms, and by the disinterested or fear driven obedience of the peoples they sought to exploit. Today It is their descendants, joined by a body of those who have subsequently risen into the elites due to their inheriting or themselves gaining some form of economic, financial, or political power, who populate national and international elite groups across the world.

An outcome being that international politician–led diplomacy has been characterised by a dysfunctional trope compounding suspicion, power, greed, and aggression. This is our heritage of international politics. Even in a simple form we can understand how symptoms of the consequent dysfunctionality can be quite easily identified in various international incidents and in their variable interpretation by the nations involved.

I want to digress to just briefly consider the idea of elite groups due to my using this concept as conceptual shorthand for the powerful national and international groupings of people that are able to deploy power, define any national interest, and also garner material and social rewards significantly beyond those of most people. Simple national-based elite groups would be constituted by different proportions of individuals drawn from top civil servants, politicians, prominent agents in the financial sector, top criminals, business-people, large land and property owners, senior members of the military and security services, religious leaders; and, as a generalization, the wealthy. Nation-based groups of these more obviously competing against each other on many inter-national affairs but perversely also cooperating to protect and advance interlinked personal interests on a global scale. At times and on certain issues they are fully aware of the value (not least in controlling national populations) of selectively emphasizing competition even with the associated risk to their own nation's well-being (indeed in a nuclear age their very existence) but they are also aware of the intertwined aspects of their personal economic interests.

Sections of these elites have been variously termed: Oligarchs (Russia, eastern Europe and China), Crony Capitalists (most obviously of sub-Saharan Africa and South America and the Far East), Aristocrats, Warlords, Mafia-type cartels and Cybercriminals, The Party, The State, the Davos class, the Business Roundtables, Heads of religions, Plutocrats, Top bankers, speculators, and Hedge fund managers; in sum the Ruling Classes as a generality.

Any specific boundary that separates an elite group from the rest is usually quite difficult to determine, unless using crude, if often perhaps instrumentally quite useful, wealth and/or power-holding position. And, as the politically reactionary philosopher Plato was aware 2,400 years ago, there has to be some capacity in any hierarchical politico/economic system for 'bright' (so potentially disruptive) individuals to ascend from the masses to the elite. Suffice to note that, even given potentially permeable masses/elite-group boundaries, there are significant barriers to joining any elite (including at least some acceptable degree of conformity to the dominant ideology); if in most countries today the ability to become wealthy in itself usually serves as an elite group ticket. It was U.S. President Eisenhower (himself an elite-group member) who on leaving office warned of the power of the Military-Industrial-Complex and the danger of its progressing its own institutional interests even where this conflicts with a wider national interest.

So elite groups progressing both institutional and personal interests as they and their precursors have more or less strongly contributed to the design and identified the purpose of any institution be it political, military, business, media, finance, criminal, intellectual, or religious. There is a considerable commonality of institutional and personal interest of those in control. And it is the control (power) aspect of elites that is of fundamental relevance for global governance and economic conditions.

As with a number of collective concepts used in this book that of 'elite' is not intended to circumscribe an easily bounded collectivity. I can't offer a ridged definition of what can seem to be an amorphous body, rigidly fixed at its core, but with an element of everchanging personal at its margins. A body that at a national level can, on very rare occasions, be subjected to revolutionary change.

Twentieth-century sociology has seen a number of attempts to define and consider elites within a debate stimulated by Marx's conception of classes and Weber's of interest-groups; with useful contributions. initially from V.Parato, G.Moscha, M.Kolabinska, and later C.Wright-Mills and T.B.Bottomore.

For the economically developed countries elite group homogeneity has included selective forms of education experienced by most elite-group members themselves and for their children. For elite-groups in the economically developing countries this aspect of elitism has been the experience of elite-groups members often being educated abroad. An exclusive education is usually but one (if very important) aspect, along with the family milieu and normative acceptance of hierarchy in any social setting, of psychological preparation for elite-group membership. This privileged intermixing also lays the basis for the accumulation of the very important 'social capital' that will help to facilitate a person's transition from privileged childhood, through gilded youth, into an elite-group power-position. A commonly implicit intention of elite group socialization being to instil a sense of justified entitlement – of any individual being a member of a privileged grouping due to some innate set of abilities (some superior faculties) rather than the set of social and economic advantages that have provided a conducive framework for their upbringing. Social intermixing, marriage, kinship obligations, and occupational networking, allow opportunities to gain reinforcement for a shared interpretation of their own experience and affirmation for their privileged position. Individuals each situated within a tangled density of interrelated social capital and economic advantages from which they can draw.

If it is difficult to define the minimum qualifications required for inclusion in any elite, the necessary conditions for membership are at least sufficiently clear for my purposes. The notion of elite will serve as a useful heuristic for understanding the operation of power in our world; and it is power than matters. I am sure that any citizen of any of the world's countries would be able to recognize the members of the elite running their own land, and so their own country's participatory ties to global power.[3]

Elite groups, representing a privileged layer of individuals located at the political, judicial, economic, criminal, and social status apex of any hierarchically stratified society, have been a defining characteristic of civil life since its inception – initially as aristocratic, religious, and military. The 19th, 20th, and 21st centuries have seen the emergence of financial, political, criminal, business, and media elites, that to some extent. have displaced the more traditional types of power holders.

I would concede that, in the absence of some system of effective bottom-up participatory governance, mass societies do need some political and administrative 'leadership'. But of more relevance to my own considerations the core issue is...... in whose interest any elite group wields the political and economic power it has been able to accumulate and so deploy.

As early as 1956 the perceptive social scientist C. Wright-Mills, referring to the US power-elite, noted that 'As the means of information and power are centralized, some men come to occupy positions in American society from which they can look down upon,

---

[3] In the African country of Tanzania, the second half of the twentieth century saw the rise of a wealthy elite popularly known as the 'wabenzi', or 'people of the Benz' due to their liking for luxury Mercedes Benz motor cars. Similar nouveau-rich groupings have arisen in many post-colonial settings –and whilst their wealth and associated conspicuous consumption is only indirectly relevant to elite control, the power they hold over both governments and national economic systems is of vital relevance.

so to speak, and by their decisions mightily affect, the everyday worlds or ordinary men and women.'

And even more so in the twenty-first century it is naked wealth rather than prestige or other forms of social status that generate power; for Raoul Martinez (2017, p224): 'The more wealth a person controls, the greater their capacity to determine the [our] future.'

If the global elite is comprised of about 5% of the population of 7/8 billion, then we have about 400 million individuals with disproportionate access to power. A significant proportion of these would be voluntarily disengaged from active participation in politics, finance, business, or the military. Such a proportion qualifying for elite group membership by wealth alone, prepared to concede control of their source of potential power (wealth) to various (institutional) investment managers; be these CEOs of companies or to managers of Hedge or other types of investment fund. Their being a leisured class of rentiers set within the wider elites. These are of little interest to my own analysis as, although they operate via a mostly parasitic relationship with society, their place in any country (especially their various tax avoidance schemes) could quite easily be reformed.

So, leaving these groups aside, we can then identify a body of about 200 million individuals. At the top of global: politics, finance, business, religious, media, crime, and the military (a seven-fold power nexus). These – the actual 'rulers of the world'- in effect interpret the past and set the political and economic conditions within which we all live.

If there is any relevance to the accusation of elite conspiracy it would be more in terms of small discrete groups (e.g. some generously funded alt-right US groups, the inner cabinet of one-party dominated states, the large Hedge and Vulture funds, religious leaders, along with co-ordinate groups of currency speculators, and in some developing countries the military cliques) rather than some interlinked process of wide-spread, internationally coordinated, planning. But if outcomes are considered we would at least be able to identify the extent of the conjunction of approach taken by sections of the global elite's quite obvious pursuance of its own self-interest. The current situation of group members experiencing similar socialization processes and having a shared (if fairly broad) social and economic ideology, means that conspiracy-type co-ordination is unnecessary as the 'hidden hand' of these 200 million individual decision-makers, designing and adjusting institutions in their perception of their own interests reveals an unplanned but convenient coordination of purpose – the not so 'hidden hand' of elite-group activities has produced a significant shift in wealth and control over the past 30- 40 years, with any improvement in the living conditions of sections of the masses being but a by-product of elite group individual and institutional activity. Direct co-ordination is unnecessary where intentionality is shared and key institutions have been designed to facilitate these intentions.

This un-conspired co-ordination receives continuous reinforcement, not just in terms of financial success but also from the collegiate/clubbable nature of family, friends, and associates, coming together – elite group members are enmeshed within a nexus of self-affirmation and specialized sense of entitlement; with the egos of leading representatives being stroked by a mass-media created sense of public admiration and normalized approval. For T.B.Bottomore (1964, p130): 'The major inequalities in society are in the main social products, created and maintained by the institutions of property and inheritance, of political and military power, and supported by particular beliefs and doctrines.'

Even as early as mid-nineteenth century Marx identified a monopoly on the control of the '......production of ideas' as being an important factor in maintaining the dominance of the ruling class. A combination of media persuasion, intellectual justification, and the tendency of populations towards obedience, have supported and provided ideas that conveniently serve elite interests. The media tends to dumb down complexity (rather than clarify this), suppresses information on viable economic and political alternatives to the status quo, and more generally takes a patronizing view of the masses.

As the neo-liberal economist Friedrich von Hayek noted (Hayek, 'The Road to Serfdom' 1944): '....the great majority are rarely capable of thinking independently ......on most questions they accept views which they find ready-made.' - a view pretty much shared with Adolf Hitler and noted in his book Mein Kampf.

For C. Wright-Mills ('The Power Elite', 1956, p4): '.....they [the 'Power Elite] are in command of the major hierarchies and organizations of modern society. They rule the big corporations. They rule the machinery of state and claim its prerogatives. They direct the command posts of the social structure, in which are now centred the effective means of the power and wealth and celebrity which they enjoy.'

A celebrity daily reinforced at the local level during their smoothed passage through the exclusive hotels, clubs, restaurants, first class air and train travel, the T.V. studios, plush conference centres, and luxury shopping outlets serving to pamper the wealthy; all emphasize their specialness, and provide some comfortable distance from the masses. They can experience the continuous flattery of a large service class closely attuned to their needs – the turned heads and admiring (if perhaps often covetous) glances of some of the public as the privileged glide by in expensive cars, yachts, and private jets. A group defined for the public more by their conspicuous consumption, and seemingly glamorous lifestyles, rather than by how they are able to fund these, and the contribution their economic and political activities might make to the wider social good.

Such is the growing dysfunctional social impact of increasing economic inequality that the wealthy increasingly seek the security and distance of gated estates, and private security groups, as parts of some cities become ever more dystopian terrains of disadvantage than the relatively integrated communities that many had once been.

But the serious issue for my own purpose is the assumed right of a relatively small number of the world's people – most of whom begin life with significant social and economic advantages, as will their own children – to wield political and/or economic power and, for what any even-handed consideration of the evidence would suggest, by progressing their own interests. My own use of the term 'elite' is as a heuristic device employed to encompass the relatively small national groups and conjoined global groupings that in effect 'rule our world'.

A significant source of division (and so evil) has been an outcome of historical events mostly re-presented in ways from the partial and narrow to the invented and malign - and these have formed the narratives of imagined injustice and oppression upon which tribal, ethnic, religious, and national hatreds have been secured - the insidious group-specific collective memories of but partial facts set in narrative contexts structured according to motivations too often projecting difference in terms of suspicion, competition, and more general antagonism.

Throughout civil history elite-groups would not have been able to deploy power to malign ends without the World's people being divided. And now I touch on a key aspect of ethnic, tribal, and national, types of group memory that is of crucial relevance to our future. Given what we know of human psychology and human history as this impacts on inter-group relations, we can be fairly confident that none of today's identifiable collectivities, be it tribe, ethnic group, clan, religion, or nation, has a history free of some legacy of evil perpetrated by its ancestors. It is extremely doubtful that human local inter-group relations have been peaceful for more than a relatively short time.

In some locations groups may have made accommodations that have at least contained inter-group violence, showing that inter-group conflict is not inevitable. Peaceful co-existence can be negotiated if conditions of agreed fairness, trust, and mutual good-will pertain. But history is replete with massacres, genocides, raiding

34

for women or other valued resources, ethnic cleansing, enslavement of others, conflict over water and over hunting territory, pastures or otherwise fertile farmland, gross economic exploitation, the destruction of neighbouring town or cities, religious conflict, and of course nation-based warfare. And this only externally directed evils – internally, few groupings have refrained from persecuting the different, the rebel, the otherwise awkward individual or minority.

The politico/economic interests of nations (as formulated by national elite groups) has been a significant determinant on how the global economic system and international political relationships have come to be constructed and so conducted – with these being competitive (economic) and conflictual (as in international political relationships).

It is of fundamental importance for the future that we recognise that indigenous peoples of all the habitable continents have been involved in on-going conflict and at times organized warfare from long before any contact with western nations. Historical events must be acknowledged but we are alive today and if the world is to work toward a peaceful future, then the contested past has to be left there. Today's conflictual issues, such as: Palestine/Israel, India/Pakistan China/Taiwan Iran/US, Russia/NATO Kurds/Turkey, Yemen, Ethiopia, Sahel, Myanmar, etc etc... need to be considered in today's forums of just global governance and assessed according to human rights and group self-determination as set out it in terms similar to the UN Charter.

The ancestors of all nations and most ethnic groups have been involved in the perpetration of evil whether as warfare, or indeed most also as in slavery. The interpretation, of facts and implications, of each conflictual event are liable to irresolvable contestation. If we want to create a peaceful World we need to move forward unhampered by an invariably contested past and assess current disputes in the context of today values about human rights and international law - accepting that the constitution and application of the latter does need reform.

If the World's people are to work towards a more peaceful future we have to accept and share the past but use it to, in a sense, begin again informed by knowing the conditions in which evil can find expression. We were not the past, we do not need to fight entrenched genealogical battles embellished and otherwise distorted by partial collective group memories. The sense of 'begin again' noted is a preparedness to frame past evils as fearsome lessons to be learned, so bracketed as an element of self-consciousness that can be overcome. The 'can' conveying a sense of optimism, of what might be achieved, is more an imperative expressing an urgent and necessary task to be taken up. There is a need to re-imagine the past as past and to live the future without variously interpreted versions of the past determining how we live together as collective units. To acknowledge that group identity can be a sustaining mode of existence for an individual – a comforting fit, with the socialized known offering emotionally enriching relationships and cultural practices – but recognizing that the types of collective identity (nation, tribe, clan, religious, and ethnic group) are in fact more often accidents of birth progressively embodied and reinforced as an outcome of intensive socialization. If we reflect closely on our existence, we can peel off the layers of personality primarily accrued from any more specific collective modes and reveal an underlying connectedness to all humanity. A connection enriched by deeply personal commitment to a willingness to transcend the socialized self and identify with the expansive potential of world-consciousness.

Historically, individuals have been but more or less significant agents in the expression of avoidable evil – key decisions are made by individuals - but it is the wider conditions within which they come to power and the national and international conditions in which they operate, that also need to be examined. If to do so would be seen as a threat by the various centres of power – financial, industrial, military, religious, dynastic, criminal, political – that have historically exercised control in the world and those that continue to do so.

We can characterize human civil history as being a 6,000 year-long journey of developing the latent awareness of how we should live together alongside a more dominant motivation seeking to fulfil baser needs realized through: domination, threat, conflict, enslavement, aggression, gaining coercive control, and other forms of exercising power over others.

A primary task must be to seek to understand the construction of circumstances that provide a context (the conditions) in which evil is more rather than less likely to be expressed – including the economic, political, and social structures within which people are socialized. The interconnecting web involving: structural inequalities and existing forms of exploitation, no realistic opportunity to find any personal fulfilment, a social environment based on aggressive competition and social status being gained for succeeding in such an environment, with economic and social structures that create and maintain class-based division, ethnic division, religious divisions, inter-nation division, polarized political division......and other such potentially divisive characteristics. Societies whose collective mindset values superficial achievement such as the mere accruing of wealth or overvalues relative achievement (in many areas including business, military, political, academic, as well as music, sport, art, entertainment) that all contribute to the dehumanization of our social relationships and to shaping our perspective on the 'others' we know of but never really know.

Immanuel Kant noted that: 'For peace to reign on Earth, humans must evolve into new beings who have learned to see the whole first."

In evolutionary terms the species Homo sapien developed from about 150,000 y.b.p. taking a more modern anatomical form about 50,000 y.b.p. In Part 1 I suggested that the underlying dynamic driving evolution is information processing. That from the very first single-cellular life-forms we can, if crudely, identify levels of development (with ideal example species obvious for each level) arranged in a hierarchy based on ability to process evermore complex patterns of information and so activate the complexity of the behavioural repertoire exhibited by species within each level. With human-beings (Homo sapien) and the level identified as 'self-consciousness' currently the species at the apex of the hierarchy.

The behaviours that characterise self-consciousness have amongst other things produced, modern medicines, legal systems, land, sea, air, and space transport, a range of other technological innovations, modern medicine, philosophy, the sciences, and other developments associated with civil life. Unfortunately, warfare was also one of these.

In terms of understanding the world and interacting with others, self-consciousness means a narrowing of view, primarily linked to personal and group interests. Self-consciousness tends towards seeing the other as friend or foe, and the foe usually being the unknown other. Self-consciousness tends towards stereotypic categorization of others, tends to notice difference rather than recognising underlying sameness, self-consciousness at home in an industrializing consumer society tends towards a focus on self rather than on common interests. Tends towards reductionist thinking; if not the generally productive reductionist analysis of the sciences - more the silo-like narrowing of, me, myself, and of my family, my tribe or group, my nation.......my 'kind', rather than more holistic thinking ('...seeing the whole...' for Kant). Generally a tendency towards essentialist and stereotypic thinking, of reducing issues to simplistic explanations often sanctioned by tradition and, in a post-modern mass society of accepting the interpretations of experts and other influential individuals whose views have a more general coherence with an individual's own intentionality; basically a tendency towards intellectual laziness and therefore a milieu that mitigates against much personal commitment to the clarification of moral implications.

Note my repeated use of the word 'tends', this indicates that the characteristics I am describing express core aspects of self-consciousness, but that at any time aspects of our next evolutionary level 'world consciousness'[4], can intrude. We can rise above the limitations of a narrow self-consciousness; tendencies can be resisted. Reflective thinking – with an assumption of rationalism and more logical considerations – can serve to provide hope for our species, that we do potentially have the psychological resources to think beyond the immediacy of self-hood and group-hood.

It is this originating, personally interpretive, aspect of our experience that offers hope for change. This capacity for creative agency (allied to the human imagination) offers the basic psychological conditions for the construction of social, economic, and political systems that can provide some humanity-affirming structures and so is our hope for humanity. Each one of us has a hold on kindness, has the potential to be in touch with our humanity. An economically comfortable upbringing in an acquisitive consumer society - with an over-emphasis on having rather than sharing, or even on being itself - can leave a child deficient in social empathy. But for most the potential to do good rather than accept evil, to get involved rather than maintain a detachment from the world, is present within the depths of our individuality. And, given the complexity and palpable flexibility of the human psyche, no human is irredeemably beyond the potential for some precocious sense of world-consciousness.

What would the evidence for the soon to appear level of 'self-consciousness' have been at the pre-Homo sapien point – this could surely only have been based on identifying the primary direction of evolution, and so a focus on the information processing model of biological adaptation. A prediction made then, and my own being made now, of a new form of 'consciousness' (self-consciousness then, and world consciousness for me), gains validity if considered in relation to the mass of biological, paleontological, and neurological evidence, showing the progressive appearance of information processing modes – action/reaction, awareness, consciousness, self-consciousness.... - in the evolutionary journey of all life on Earth.

I suggest that the past offers persuasive empirical support for a future evolutionary stage/mode expressed as 'world consciousness', equivalent to the development of the taxonomic family Hominidae from Homo erectus to Homo sapien. This being a development that would allow us to aspire to economic, political, and social

---

[4] This next level is of course offered as a notional idea – and it might be that the species Homo sapien becomes extinct prior to fully attaining the 'world conscious' level.

relationships beyond the competitive, the conflictual, and the more generally evil. That we can use the concept of world consciousness, and its potential for moral enlightenment as it transcends the self-conscious mode, to stimulate the design of economic and political institutions that would sustain humanity into its future.

If it has taken about 1.8 million years since the first Homo forms of consciousness evolved from earlier some Homo erectus primates, then the 50,000 odd years from the appearance of modern Homo-sapien down to the past 6,000 years of the development of more mature forms of civil life, then surely even another 1,000 years for a more definite transition towards 'world-consciousness' would seem to be reasonable. But only if the mode of self-consciousness that dominates today's world does not lead to the early eradication of life on Earth; a distinct possibility.

We cannot identify a specific biological transition point between each of the four crude modes of information processing noted above – but using a metaphor involving a colour, say red gradually changing to brown as the wavelength of radiation is adjusted. If normal colour vision, we would quite easily see the distinction between red and brown but as we observe the original redness fade and the brown gradually being revealed, the point somewhere between the two when we can say that the change actually occurs would be quite difficult to identify – although each end would be clear. Unless, that is, we chose to identify colour (red or brown) by a specific wavelength. But even choosing this quantifiable point would still be a subjective decision, as would any attempt to identify a specific primate species whose information processing capacity is assessed to be a new form of 'awareness' becomes 'consciousness' or 'consciousness' becomes 'self-consciousness.' Each progressive mode of information processing subsumes some primary characteristics of the preceding modes and some individuals in each mode show precocious behavioural aspects of the next.

The pre-Homo sapien development of self-consciousness can be traced by the increasing sophistication of tool manufacture over about 2 million years and by skull (brain) development (especially the 'bulge' just behind the left-hand eye socket related to speech) – both aspects of evolutionary development appearing from species such as Homo habilis (circa. 2 m.y.b.p), and more modern forms of Homo erectus down to Homo neanderthalensis and Homo sapien.

I acknowledge that what has (perhaps up to the time of the innovations of numeracy and literacy) been primarily biological evolution - assessed in relation to information processing capacity - became increasingly more complex, in that, as a species we have an information processing capacity significantly enlarged;

supplemented by having the underlying form of biological evolution overlaid by humankind's intellectual achievements, as increasingly aided by the technological developments that have been central aspects of civil life. Biological evolution became overlain with civil development (with its production and accumulation of knowledge), and the progressive intensification of this being compounded by IT-based information processing; with today all three woven together as they each contribute to the expanding Reality within which humankind exists.

In the twenty-first century, the power of IT-based information processing is a key driver of the development of civilization, in ways qualitatively different to past technological innovations. So whereas I am here positing my concept of world-consciousness as being in the progressive line of: stimulus/response, pre-conscious, conscious, and self-conscious, evolutionary modes, I do need to acknowledge that this is a gross simplification. We can identify 'ideal' species (forms) for each of these modes but between each of these are thousands (possibly millions) of species exhibiting more of an incremental progression than clear points of separation. But the idea of 4/5 primary modes of information processing is useful to illustrate the bio-teleological potential for humankind - especially in relation to reducing the evil in the world – one with a range of practical scientific, and some profoundly philosophical, implications.

I am not suggesting that this is a connection to some biologically inevitable process of evolving consciousness - the stark epistemological reality is that it is a dubious assumption to conclude that evolution has a direction, some pre-determined teleology related to a particular species; that it is inextricable drawn towards some end-state. As I have been endeavouring to show, we can trace a progression in terms of information processing capacity, but a continuing place in this for humankind is not inevitable - any species can become extinct and so its information processing capacity becomes irrelevant, becomes but an aspect of the overall evolutionary lineage. The concept of bio-teleological merely reflects the direction expressed by the evolutionary dynamic of increasing information processing capacity.

World-consciousness, as I have outlined it, is a direction for humanity that challenges the evils of human self-conscious history to not be repeated – for modern humans, a 50,000 odd year tale of the increasing expression of evil. World-consciousness is a possible direction for humanity, and only in this sense is teleological, the extent to which we align our lives with the implications of this possibility is the extent to which we are living morally authentic lives.

We humans as individuals, groups, nations, and as a species, might appeal to some personalized god, some idea of the entry requirements for eternal bliss, or some range of human ideals for guidance on how to behave. But I believe that the information processing mode of 'world-consciousness' can only evolve (find expression in the world) if we, each of us as individual human beings - in an act of reflective authenticity – decide that world-consciousness is a morally based mind-set to be fostered by today's individuals - it is an expression of moral autonomy at its most critical.

As a slight digression to consider a more metaphysical implication of my positing information process of adaptation to an ever-expanding Reality.......just imagine the cognitive capability of the type of organism that would evolve into anatomically modern Homo sapien circa 50,000 y.b.p. .....perhaps of some primate species one million years ago? How much could they have 'known' beyond their immediate geographic locality and emotion-laden relations within their small primate social groups? Can you grasp the implications of the information dynamic model? The very emergence of Homo sapien from an earlier primate species was one of those implications!

Individuals of that pre-Homo sapien primate species might occasionally have gazed up at the stars with some primitive sense of curiosity, and some obviously did start manipulating materials (stone, bone, and wood,) in what we came to recognize as tool usage – but just consider the difference in cognitive ability and imaginative world-view between advancing primates species over just the past 1 million years to realize what might be possible over the 1 million years to come. Just how much will they (some intelligent species of the future) 'know' about say the Universe; or indeed how will they know in terms of metaphysics more generally? I am not just suggesting some accumulation of knowledge by our own (aided by computer-based technology) species but rather what will in fact be a new super-intelligent (by our own standard) biological species; if possibly one evolved from our own.

Or will some self-replicating A.I. entity have by then taken over the leading information-processing role, with any surviving humans (in the unlikely event that our own species can survive such a scenario) living on the margins of some super-intelligence dominated world; surviving due to their presence being irrelevant to the dominant information-processing forms that had displaced them.

A third alternative for 1 million years hence could be a planet denuded of the means to support any form of intelligent life due to humans long having destroyed themselves, presumably by some combination of nuclear conflagration and/or environmental degradation.

An A.I. takeover is a realistic possible scenario, as is the end of all intelligent life on Earth, but for now humankind holds its future in its own hands. How we order the world by taking a necessary global perspective on economic planning, environmental protection, and on governance, requires urgent consideration. In all three areas we seem to be on route to disaster......and this within but 50-100 years – a potentially terminal disaster brought about by our inability to move beyond the narrow parameters characteristic of the self-conscious level of decision-taking – towards what I term self-consciousness in order to capture the sense of the global perspective required.

Being human in its-self is not a pathological condition - The uniqueness of individuality is a fundamental opportunity to 'be'. For some this be-ing is in suffering, for others in creative becoming, and for most be-ing in a more 'mundane' sense from which we can each seek to develop our own level of consciousness. That the tendency towards evil can be eased by the realization of more transcendentally possible ways of living together.

As individuals and as collectives we humans tend towards expressing a mix of behaviours, at worst we would term these our colluding in evil – wars, massacres, raping, enslaving, killings, ethnic cleansing, and gross economic exploitation. During more enlightened times people have been aware of this raw tendency and of the need to maintain a level of social order. So public institutions have been devised to mitigate our more anti-social behaviours. These institutions have included systems of representative governance, of legal codes, religious and secular moral injunctions, and of economic arrangements seeking to balance different interests within a wider context of consensual acceptance. Internationally, I would highlight the United Nations and the range of human rights guidelines that it has generated as the global institutional, if too often seriously flawed in operation, modern expression of humankind's collective ethical wisdom.

The twenty-first century Reality is now so vast in terms of information (especially knowledge content), and its rate of expansion so great, that humankind as a species risks being terminally overwhelmed as it becomes unable to assimilate the more material and technological impact on such aspects of Reality as: the biosphere, the human implications of the internet, consumerism, the armaments industry, and robotics and automation more generally. The elusive, uneasy, complexity of the 'liquid modernity' noted by Zygmund Baumann.

So much information pouring over and through us, eroding the relatively more secure psychological foundations of the relatively more stable traditional. Our psychological constitution has over centuries generated an interrelated uber-complexity of discovery and invention. But with each human being born anew with a psychological constitution showing little progress in cognitive capacity on the human born 20,000 years ago – a mismatch between what we can now do (technologically) and our seeming inability to manage the consequences. A mismatch possibly revealing the conditions for an evolutionary dead-end and so extinction for our species. Invention has accumulated, as has complexity, whereas wisdom has remained static (if certain moral truths retain a continuing relevance) – as a species we are struggling to manage technology in sustainable, human-sense ways. Some, such as Arthur Koestler, have described this mismatch in terms of brain physiology, highlighting the lack of functional integration between the 'more intelligent' neo-cortex and the 'more emotional' central areas (older in evolutionary terms) of the brain.

In terms of universal values, in the context of managing the urgent problems facing the world, we need some agreed set of human values. Those already outlined in the Charter of the United Nations could provide a good base for the constitution of global governance. Experience of the UN suggests that interpreting the provisions of the Charter in terms of actual practice would, given the current arrangements of that body, be susceptible to variable self-interested motivations of governments and the globally powerful elites. But we can at least imagine comprehensively reformed UN forums serving as potentially useful interpretive bodies for the application of the Charter's provisions. Forums ideally composed of individuals that have a proven record of non-factional wisdom. How this qualification can be assessed is another complex challenge, some others include being to determine to what extent individual nations would be prepared to cede sovereignty (a base-line necessary condition for effective global governance), and what would be the scope for sectional lobbying and public representations to such a body.

We are not necessarily discussing a World Government here – just a global body established to apply even-handed wisdom to complex social and political issues, as guided by the provisions of the UN Charter; a globally-appropriate level of governance designed to address global-wide issues. Two primary factors led to the UN Charter being initially drawn up, one positive the other less so. Positively, it was a response by the heads of leading nations to public demand for something to prevent yet another drift into the experience of warfare following the deaths of over 100m in WWs I and II. More cynically, I would suggest that at the time when the UN's aims were established in their perceptively enlightened ('world conscious') form, agreement was reached due to the world's most powerful nations knowing that they could use these when deemed necessary to condemn the action of other nations and ignore (or artfully relativize) them if they were critical of their own actions. The lack of a willingness to cede sovereignty to the new body and the previous experience of international diplomacy (especially the LoN and the Kellog-Briand Pact) made this a certainty, one repeatedly and depressingly confirmed by the subsequent development of the UN.

But the cynical, self-interested actions of nations making up the body of the UN should not detract from the inspirational nature of the Charter's provisions; indeed the Charter stands as a written monument to humankind's collective enlightenment that would shame the subsequent actions of national leaders. (see the Appendix 3 below for some tentatively drafted ideas for a re-imagined, re-constructed, UN.)

In terms of power on a global level, the assumed authority of nation-states to represent the interest of the populations of the 193 full member-states of the UN is illusory. And this without even considering the extent to which nation-statehood itself actually represents the interests or even the wishes of each nation's population, rather than those of the elite groups who in effect run these countries. The primary 'global interest' is surely peaceful co-existence between and within nations.

Leaving this fundamental question aside, I want instead to focus here on global 'governance'. The concept of global governance (rather than global government) better captures the purpose of designing and introducing a layered system of administration able to operationalise how best the peoples of our world can live together – ideally sharing resources in a world with improving environmental and fairer economic conditions, and one avoiding wars and minimising other forms of conflict. The concept of government suggests static representation and assumed power, whereas governance assumes on-going interrogation and a more dynamic approach to co-existence.

Governance suggests design (implying purpose) and invites continuous questioning on any system's value and possible scope for improvements – the best form of governance would be enlightened by a sense of purpose and any related political system would be but a supplementary means of operationalising this.

Nation-states have been constructed out of political and social processes and so can in theory be deconstructed and remodelled; or indeed global governance could be designed without the divisive presence of nation-states (of a tier of nation-statehood). Perhaps a world without countries would be more of a longer-term ambition than immediately realizable, especially given the nation-based enculturalization currently being experienced by most of the world peoples.

The conflictual tropes generated to advance elite group interests currently pervading international relations should give way to the language of negotiation, within a wider context that assumes a global interest in peace and co-operation. The mass media and populist politician's terminology – mostly sourced from the xenophobic movie industry, the comic book, the barroom and on the sports-field - and the mendacious language of diplomacy, must be set aside to allow space for the language of negotiation, understanding, and mutual co-operation. And these set within a framework prioritising justice and peace. The forum for the coming together of would-be antagonists must include some judicial/political body tasked with framing issues within a wider global constitution. A constitution not dissimilar to that set out in the UN charter – but unlike that one, a constitution, determinedly infusing international relations rather than being some set of abstract ideas retained as but a residue of some more enlightened expression of hope only invoked as but another source of assumed linguistic support to justify actions to advance short-sighted national interests. Another layer of deracinated verbiage deployed to veil the hegemonic geopolitics that currently pertains.

If a fair and inclusive system of world governance, based on some tiers of genuine participatory democracy, were ever to be established, it would need to be alert to attempts made by disaffected elite group members seeking to return to sovereign nation-statehood by undermining global unifying processes. And the natural inclination of genuine participatory democracy, in relation to communication and the sharing of ideas, will open-up the space for this. The only realistic option would be (if the curtailing of valued freedoms of expression is to be avoided): the efficient management of administration, obviously open and uncorrupted governance, and continuous vigilance. All in order to continuously prove and promote its worth.

But in the anarchic terrain of global communications it does seem that the promotion of dangerous/harmful ideas and obviously false claims ('alternative facts') would require some open media-editing process. Ideally, this would be undertaken by a respected body operating separately from government as it interprets pre-establish guidelines that had been arrived at following a public debate informed by multiple perspectives (so participatory democracy), tending towards openness and inclusivity, on what was acceptable to be shared in any relevant public space. Guidelines to be regularly revisited in order to amend if required in response to ongoing social and technological developments.

Is humanity destined to trudge relentlessly and sightless towards its extinction as a species, or can we find an alternative? Any alternative can realistically only be viable if national interests are seen to align to some transcendental aims infusing global economic and political justice and the interests of future generations.

Robust alternatives to nation-state driven hegemony can realistically only be based on the recognition of a shared 'international interest' requiring the need to cede sovereignty in areas of primary international concern – be these economic, environmental, or in terms of conflict. National interests encompassed within an intentional milieu of mutual respect and genuine co-operation, expressed in a language of unity and collective hope. The intentional element determining global governance should discard elite determined notions of national interest and replace these with governance in the interest of our children and the generations that we hope will follow.....and will do so in peace.

We can note six necessary conditions for international peace:

- Fundamental reform of the UN.
- Committing to the terms of the UN Charter (as a Constitution).
- Accepting the authority of those charged to interpret the Charter in relation to particular issues – so agreeing to accept any 'rulings/decisions', perhaps with a right to appeal?
- Nations ceding sovereignty over key issues, including the right to threaten or wage war.
- A sufficient proportion of the global population committed to a new enlightened form of governance.
- The willingness of each community, be this nation state, religious sect, ethnic group, etc.to concede that few if any such communities have a history entirely free from some form of aggressive action against others. And to be prepared to eschew historic antagonisms and, in a sense begin again. To build a new form of world governance rather than retain the festering and invariably contested claims of past injustice.

Those elements which differentially contribute to forming any particular (individual, group, tribe, nation) perspective are not fixed, they are more tendencies towards interpretations, and as such are socially constructed. Historically influenced as but a part of any current elite-group's interpretive framework. But human beings have the ability, more a constant liability, to reflect. And it is within this reflective capacity where lies the potential to transcend the socialized circumscription of our approach towards understanding our own lives.

Consideration of humanity's conflictual history would reveal its extent and complexity. The extent being the destruction of built and natural environments, and of millions of people whose lives have been ended prematurely. As to complexity, we would be confronted with the challenge of identifying causes and of fairly apportioning blame. The solidly sticky strands of evil have trailed remorselessly through human civil history. What is pretty obvious is that few if any group of peoples living today, whether nations, religions, tribes, or other can honestly claim that their ancestors have been entirely innocent.

Even in crude religious terms: Hindus have killed Moslems, Moslems have killed Hindus, Buddhists have killed, and been killed by each of these and also by Christians who have also killed and been killed by Moslem, Hindus and Buddhists. And those without any religion have killed all of those with a religion and have been killed by each of these. A veritable melting pot of killing of the 'different' by the 'different.' Even groups that have suffered awful treatment during the 20th and 21st centuries alone have ancestors that have been involved in the most evil of actions.

- Armenians ......have been involved in killing Turkish Moslems.
- Kurds have been involved in killing Armenians
- The Jews during the synthetic formation of their nationhood murdered those already living in what were, for the group self-identified as Jews, a land promised to them by their god (Yahweh)
- Uighurs have raided across border regions of China in the past.
- Ukrainians massacred Poles during WWII (1943)

Just a few examples of the ancestors of the oppressed having themselves been oppressors.

Are there some aspects of human nature that would invariably lead to conflict? Or has conflict more simply been due to rational assessments made by people/leaders seeking to enhance their own group's access to valued resources? Some more rational cost benefit analysis determining irrational action. Irrational when considered in terms of the harms associated with evil acts. If we are to design the form of international relations in ways that mitigate such evils we would need to set some agreed standards and then design in the conditions for their application. This latter has been the ongoing problem with peace treaties and non-aggression pacts since the dawn of civil life shown most obviously in the 20th century failure of the Lon and the UN to prevent between nation conflict. We do know that today's international political and economic institutions have to a significant extent been designed to favour the narrow interests of elite groups.

Part III

'The spirit is smothered, as it were by ignorance, but so soon as ignorance is destroyed, spirit shines forth, like the sun when released from clouds.......We must dare to invent the future.'

Thomas Sankara

I noted at the start of this extended essay that as individuals we in a sense 'find ourselves' within existence – most of us experience consciousness as of ourselves within and the others, and the world more generally, as being out there – a external source of the information realised as personal experience. Many of us in more affluent countries are fortunate enough to grow up in fairly benign family and social settings, feeling loved and being loving. An almost cocoon-like period of childhood but one that becomes ever more infiltrated by awareness of the harsh facts of the world beyond our more immediate circumstances. The realization that other children's lives are degraded by poverty, hunger, poor housing, and medical care, as refugees and being more directly involved in the horrors of civil or inter-nation conflict. Children forced into crime, prostitution, begging, garbage-picking or sweated labour, just in order to survive from day-to-day. So many of the world's children growing up in fear-inducing conditions, painfully aware of the poverty of their circumstances.....that they are but the detritus of civil life.

It is difficult to avoid the images of others suffering seen on TV/smart phone/iPad – and these only the surface of global suffering that those in control of the mass media choose to show. We increasingly become aware of just how difficult are the lives of many other of the World's peoples.

But why should I feel that I have any responsibility towards others beyond my family, class, tribe, caste, country...etc? Why should I not just get on with my own relatively comfortable life? In some ways I do just get on with my daily life but a core part of me is aware that we - as in all people in the world - need fundamental change in the ways in which the international economic system and the international political institutions operate. My earlier book 'The Human Condition' (Dyer, 2021) included an analysis of aspects of the global economic system before going on to tentatively suggest how the system could be redesigned in ways that would: end life-threatening poverty, reduce economic inequality, provide opportunity, and maintain environmental sustainably. This present text has focused much more on international political institutions – accepting that the current economic arrangements strongly influence the conditions for international politics.

The 'we' that have a need for change is not just an appeal to help the poorest, most exploited, most oppressed, in the world, or to introduce a bit more economic justice in terms of equality of opportunity..... No the 'we' is all of us, those on the crude scale ranging from the poorest to the richest and all those in between. Without comprehensive change in the economic system and the international political institutions the future of the whole of humanity is threatened. Relentless environmental degradation threatens the mid-to-longer term viability of the planet as a habitat for human beings. And of more immediate concern, the sightless behemoth of the conflict industry progressively accelerates the world towards warfare potentially involving a significant exchange of thermonuclear devices.

The suggestion that we 'find ourselves within existence' – implies the finding of the already there as well as the realization that most of us have the agency to transcend the limitations of the socialization processes that we have experienced. Being prepared to stand exposed to our own reflective self, a mode of self-hood informed by profound consideration of a life sub-specie eternities. I am suggesting that we have an existential responsibility to purposefully decide on how we should live, not in term of personal career, close relationships, day to day attitudes, etc (although these would also probably come to be involved) but a deeper level of considering our lives in the context of humanity itself rather than the individual as myself.

There is a correspondence between perspective-taking on your own life within Reality in terms of self-creative engagement with a future involving others – the cognitive bridge to world-consciousness - and the key task of endeavouring to take-up the perspective of the other in relation to this situation or that issue. Each requires us to adopt processes determined to transcend two aspects of our individuality, the first the individual as socialized, the second as an individual prepared to assume a level of social responsibility beyond their more immediate relationships; and each of these as processes of open-ended engagement. Both directed towards transcendence – moving beyond the narrowness of the accidentally socialized and of the limitations of self-consciousness.

In our personal lives we can feel a depressing sense that there is an ontological absurdity in the very fact of our existence. The world is so unjust – some born into comfortable lives some born into the misery of poverty – some dying young, some living into old age. Most of us uneasy with trying to find some sense of purpose beyond material ambitions.

Our cries for justice and peace echo around an unresponsive universe. The immensities of space and time magnify my own helplessness, my aloneness. When we consider our flickering existence in the silent immensities within which our lives are set, we can quite easily lapse into despair. To seek some solace in family, work, hobbies, in the distractions of entertainment, or try to obtain some comfort in the superficial satisfaction of material goods and services so pressingly available for those with sufficient income.

My own life has been felt as an investigative journey seeking answers to the injustices so obvious in the world; the 20th/21st century's bounteous expression of evil. I progressed from curious childhood to questioning and angry young adulthood to more reflective, if still angry middle age. And throughout this journey having progressively formed a strong sense of what needs to be done to end, or at least significantly mitigate, the expression of evil in our world.

The primary conditions, reflecting directly upon each one of us, is to accept the relative conditions of our lives in local social settings – those experienced within a family, class, caste, religion, ethnic or other group, nation, etc. More often the source of our prejudices and stereotypes, the formation of our general outlook and more specific interpretive frameworks within the psychological processes involved in our socialization – i.e. the accidental setting of our within existence. We need to accept this randomly experienced lived relativity but to seek to transcend it in order to acknowledge our singular collective species identity within humanity more generally. To foster an outlook that prioritizes issues such as poverty, inequality, environmental sustainability, justice, and conflict......facing humanity as a collective.

Consider each of our own genealogies – reverse engineer our own unique presence in the world - the very incalculable (statistically improbable) odds against you or I ever existing. And even more so of our experiencing our being in the here and now.

Let's leave aside the metaphysical perspective involving the very improbability of life itself – that profound mystery of why humanity is here at all. But rather than this let's consider how our ancestors negotiated our ignorance of the 'meaning' of our existence......that enigmatic mystery that the religions have each attempted to explain using ideas imagined by some people at some time long ago, those who compiled the various 'holy' texts: Bible, Koran, Torah, Vedas, Tripitaka, Kojiki, Guru Granth Sahib, Avesta, etc.

Authors of these texts assumed that they lived on a flat earth circled by the Sun, whose sky was but a material cover beyond which was a bright light glimpsed through star-shaped 'pinholes' in the fabric of the sky.

The sacred texts were written for people whose ancestors had relied on 'hope' to manage the emotional dissonance invoked by consideration of the many difficult and dangerously unpredictable vicissitudes of pre and early historic lives that they were liable to encounter on an almost daily basis. From hope, allied to imagination, came the gods – even the mystery of death could be re-imagined from hope, as but a continuation of life in some other form, if only for the 'chosen'. Those peoples whose gods were often depicted by those who wrote the holy texts from their imaginations, and for their own purposes, as often cruel and always demanding. Their being able to induce awe in believers by claims of acts and miracles that suspended the laws of nature as we came to learn about them and demanding of total obedience. Gods whose earthly representatives required social elevation, and for most quite generous material rewards.

So setting aside the substantial 'why at all' of life, and also hope allied to imagination producing the religious attempts to resolve the mystery of the meaning of life..... What we do know is that our planet was formed from rotating cosmic dust-clouds about 4.5 billion years ago. By some particular combination of its position (distance from the Sun, rotational speed) and material and climatic conditions it provided just the circumstances suitable for chemical complexity to increase to a critical point when we can judge that 'life' on earth had begun.

These 'Goldilocks' conditions are predicted to also be a feature of numerous planets elsewhere in the universe. Recent (2013) calculations, using up-to-data, suggest that possibly up to 10% of the 100 billion star systems within just our own Milky Way Galaxy could provide conditions potentially suitable for life to have evolved – This is of course quite speculative (not in terms of the conditions, but more in terms of likelihood of any life actually beginning) and simple life is one phenomenon, with civil life being something much more complex.

The Earth has seen life from about 3.8 billion years ago, with the simplest of cells (Prokaryotes) appearing from about 3.5 billion years ago, and then more complex cells (Eukaryotes) from about 1.6 billion years ago – then with multi-cellular life evolving in evermore complex ways, following an adaptational dynamic based on the development of organisms able to process increasingly complex forms of information.

Some type of nervous system is the primary means by which an organism engages within its environment as it processes incoming information streaming from the environment and processes a selection (each species has its own informational 'bandwidth') of this internally; with species-specific behaviour being the most obvious outcome. We can see quite easily the advance in information processing ability if we compare any species of the genus paramecium (evolved approx. 715 m.y.b.p.) with a human-being (evolved approx. 150,000 y.b.p., as already noted, to a 'modern' from about 50,000 years ago). The paramecium is a single-celled creature that uses up about 50% of its total available energy output in moving around in its watery habitat. Fortunately, being a grazer (on algae, bacteria, and yeasts) and not a hunter, it does not have to move too far or too quickly. It is a single-celled organism without any neuron-based 'nervous system' but with its primary behaviours.....of movement, grazing, and digestion, being coordinated via a macronucleus with a micronucleus controlling reproduction and the passing on of genetic material to the next generation. Then compare this to the species Homo sapiens with its approx. 86 billion neuron-based nervous system potentially sensitive to millions of bits of information continuously streaming in from its habitat. A stream from which information is selected (mostly auto-consciously), which is then processed, consciously and unconsciously, within the organism. Unlike the paramecium, we can realistically describe human information processing as involving intentions, motivations, memories, emotions, plans, and other concepts embodied in the description of the human psychological system. The resultant behaviours being significantly more complex than those of the simpler organism – a human being can walk, run, jump, dance, swim, and even fly in machines that members of the species have invented and constructed, it can perform complex surgery, read a map, invent the internal combustion engine, the particle accelerator, the computer, the wheelbarrow, tin cans and the tin opener, can travel to the moon and beyond – it can also kill and devise the means of doing so in forms unimaginable even but 100 years ago.

So, we now find ourselves on a planet that has proved to be conducive for complex information-processing based life to evolve, within a universe that possibly provides similar conditions for other conscious lifeforms. The bio-mechanisms of evolution also offer another source of our uniqueness as individuals. Humans reproduce by two individuals coming together to blend an egg (ovum) with a sperm – and in a traditional setting this would take place during a body-on-body act of intercourse between a female and a male. So firstly, we need to have two people whose lives intersect and who also find each other sufficiently attractive to undertake this act (accepting the act of rape). The two that do – our parents – were but two in billions that could, at least theoretically have formed a mating couple. So having the parents we do have (and being gifted but a tiny quite random selection of the total genetic material they each had available) is an initial source of a coincidental uniqueness for many of us. If we then consider that in a 25 year period of fertility a female could produce between 300 – 400 eggs and a single male ejaculation (about a teaspoon, 2-5 ml, of semen) can contain up to 200 – 500 million sperm – such is the exuberance of nature - the odds of our having the very specific genetic constitution that we do have is quite awesome. All these stages of material and organic processes involving a genealogy of randomness, possibility, coincidence, and I would add an underlying mystery, contribute to the biological constitution of each one of us.

Rather than being overwhelmed by an awareness of these sources of our this uniqueness, or simply just ignoring our material and genealogical heritage and getting on with life, I feel a strong sense of responsibility – my uniqueness is a fundamental source of my autonomy, and exercising my autonomy makes me stand forth – not stand out, as if seeking elevation above others – but stand forth having reflected deeply on how I should live in this world in a way that transcends the relativity of the accidental circumstances (in terms of place and time, and so social setting) of my presence ....here and now. Our sense of self comes from within and enwraps us as we grow into adulthood – our individuality is sourced in our awareness exposed to what we experience.

I would urge you to assume responsibility linked to the opportunity that your uniqueness and a life to be lived in the here and now has gifted you to seek to transcend your own social setting, and to thoughtfully reflect on how we can together seek to improve the world for the whole species of Homo sapien. Although 'improve' suggests a modest amount of reform, whereas the improvement required to achieve a world without conflict would be significant. Requiring, in effect, a fundamental resetting of the conditions of international relations. To move away from today's conditions of international relationships based on hegemonic economic competition and political conflict to one based on co-operation and peaceful co-existence.

An individual human life might be simply expressed as being but a '...sigh between two eternal silences' (noted earlier in this essay) but as the connection we each have to humankind as a collective entity, generation following generation, we are part of an ongoing evolutionary phenomenon. Let's collectively endeavour to ensure that this '......sigh between two eternal silences' is not the fate of humankind as an entire species, on but a longer timescale – to be self-consciously driven to extinction.

A fundamental aspect of our lives inextricably involves the idea of reflective choice, and this in the context of accepting the responsibility that accompanies this sense of agency – an important aspect of being what it 'feels like' to be human. An aspect of existence effectively denied to individuals of any other species. And this potential for individuality, for some sense of being an autonomous agent, is the step we can make between unreflective conformity and the post-reflective personal decision-making on how we should live. Within this self-directed personal narrative a thread of authenticity can emerge to be woven into a life of moral substance.

My giving priority to the concept of authenticity as an existential aspiration is intended to express some deeper connection to all the potential good that inheres within the human condition. Authenticity as a form of transcendent achievement realized as an outcome of world-consciously directed engagement with life. The lived outcome of a decision to assume a fundamental level of personal responsibility for the implications of the mystery of finding oneself in existence. The question...... authentic in relation to what? Stands out.... bear with me.

I have traced the rise of consciousness in terms of the increasing potential to process evermore information and I point to human self-consciousness as being an advanced embodiment of this ability. Human history shows that the gross expression of evil has been a fearsome and bleak feature running through the social processes and political institutions that have characterized civilizations associated with self-consciousness. But another aspect of civil life has been the refinement of morality, given a symbolic and ordered form in scriptural commands, civil laws (codes - injunctions), and in collectively stated aims informed by enlightened humanistic aspirations. In relation to these types of codified (formalized) morality - in the context of world consciousness - we now have various human rights acts and I have highlighted the UN's collective version of these as set out in its charter. A charter that can embody hope for the human species.

Since the earliest time of civil life some of humankind's political and religious leaders have been able to outline the types of ethical code that we should adhere to - and this offers a glimmer of genuine hope. The problem throughout history being that the tensions between abstract moral priorities and particular issues where vested interests are challenged have almost always been resolved to the detriment of morality and in favour of narrow-minded self-interest. Most often the interests of powerful elites (if with the obedient compliance of the masses) and this in the pursuit of wealth, land, or increasing power. The interests supporting war have tended to be stronger than those endeavouring to make the case for peace, the distribution of the material benefits of civil life have tended to favour various types of elite group that have been able to obtain power and who have had no compunction in using it to benefit themselves. Mostly to the short-term detriment of the masses and the long- term detriment of all.

We can characterize human civil history as being a 6,000 year-long journey of developing the latent awareness of how we should live together alongside a more dominant motivation seeking to fulfil baser needs realized through: domination, coercion, threat, conflict, enslavement, aggression, various types of institutional control, and other forms of exercising power over others.

Let's see if I can do a bit more with the concept of authenticity on an individual level because without the engagement of committed and determined individuals the systemic tendencies towards the expression of evil are more likely to prevail. Striving for authentic understanding, and to act authentically in ones encounter with-in existence, means being 'honest' in the best possible sense i.e. existentially rather than only legally. Honest as in being true to certain self-formulated ideas, gained during the profoundly personal solitude of self-reflection, to take responsibility for one's own life – an unconditional commitment to seek existential truth. Trying, whenever possible, to go beyond surface understanding and explanations, and also to attempt to separate your own self-interests and potential for bias from your commenting about or understanding any contested issue. It does not mean that you should be seeking to eradicate personal and intellectual bias[5], it just means you should endeavour to acknowledge these, take them into account, and ensure that any bias (which is a natural propensity) is regularly subject to open scrutiny.

Authenticity is intimately related to personal and intellectual integrity. It is about how each of us in our individuality looks life with its multi-shifting complexity, dangers, joy and sadness, and the ontic absurdity of our lives that the writer Albert Camus so clearly drew

---

[5] Bias can be the outcome of accumulated experience and allows a necessary short-hand understanding of issues – but when these are contentious then the matter of bias, and the need for a deeper consideration/analysis comes to the fore.

attention to, squarely in the 'eye'. Trying to be authentic, and searching for authenticity in our understanding, is the thread of humanity running throughout our task of facing absurdity, with its uncomfortable existential implications. On the personal level to stand-forth, determined to live rightly in relation to the human values that have been revealed; not least by a number of past and present religious leaders and secular thinkers in both the 'East' and the 'West'. And on the intellectual level to strive for deeper understanding, valuing the power of rational thinking, ever prepared to genuinely reconsider your views in response to the reasoned arguments or suggestive insights of others, or of new information becoming available.

Finally, being personally authentic, and searching for intellectual authenticity, is to be prepared to follow the implications of experience to its core and to accept responsibility for one's own involvement. Thomas Nagel wrote in relation to the absurd: 'What he [Camus] recommends is defiance or scorn. We can salvage our dignity, he appears to believe, by shaking a fist at the world which is deaf to our pleas, and continuing to live in spite of it. This will not make our lives un-absurd, but it will lend them a certain nobility.' For Nagel, Camus's is a '...romantic and slightly self-pitying' view. But the insight that allows us to understand the absurd nature of human lives highlights the limits of the human condition, for Nagel, knowing this: '......we can approach our absurd lives with irony instead of heroism or despair.' (Nagel, 1979, pp.22-23)

For myself, the process of confronting the seeming absurdity of our lives, reveals the fundamental nature of moral concerns – we come to the conclusion of absurd via a comparison of a world of random unjust circumstances for some and equally random unjustified good fortune for others – and of course, to the lack of any reply to our cries of despair about this......the world just continues to enigmatically turn, trailing evil as it does so. We must aim to create a sense of a moral nobility by acknowledging the absurd but seeking to transcend this by assuming a life lived in defiance of its seemingly depressing finality, brushing its negative (nay saying) implications aside – it merely serving as a stimulus to our overcoming its pessimistic contaminants. The absurd is not a conclusion. It is but a provisional assessment, denying the continuing personal realization (as authentic) of our confronting evil, and also an assessment lacking the consciousness raising potential inherent within evolving humankind.

We must be prepared to risk exposure to the full blast of a Reality that constantly buffets the limited certainties to which we cling, as individuals and humankind, like shipwrecked mariners might desperately cling onto drift-wood. The touch-stone of 'human values' – is a key source of an authentic perspective, authentic because these would be values formulated following a reflective consideration of the circumstances of a person's life - as a wider guiding intentional framework from which one's attitude in relation to each particular issue is drawn. The extent to which these align expresses the authenticity of a person's life. Each person commits to their own conscience-driven values as they progress the interrogation of a moral basis for their own lives. The conditions for authenticity include: clarity of values (and the implications of these for a person's life), personal autonomy, critical self-reflection, consistency, but most of all in assuming responsibility.

As I approach the end of this essay it will be of value to consider the concept of 'reason' (or rational thinking), a concept synonymous with the best work in philosophy. How best (most effectively in relation to purpose) to apply the organizing framework of reason is probably the most useful thinking process to arise from philosophical speculation. I would argue that it is only of any real use when it is aligned to the realities of everyday life and that the representations generated are accessible to any person motivated to make some effort.

Reason could be described as the 'guided seeking for understanding', guided by the intellect in relation to a purpose; there are good or bad purposes but ideally reason initially aims at a neutral evaluation of the facts arising from the consideration of any subject matter. The concept of reason expresses the ability of humans to interrogate and interpret an issue in particular ways. Involving assessing the veracity of facts and clarifying relationships between these, the justification of any associated claims, examining the logical consistency of arguments, and identifying the implications of judgements and suggested actions. Reason has its own determinants of intellectual acceptability that can allow explanations and arguments to be set out or challenged within a mode of credibility. The expectation of intellectual acceptability running throughout reasoning processes, especially in relation to conflictual issues, is the best means humans have to gain an understanding of any issue but also for seemingly competing views to be debated in terms of facts and implications – if these debates must necessarily have to take place within a background context of agreed ethical parameters (some presumption).

Even a cursory glance through human civil history and its accumulated results can induce despair – the mostly seemingly rational expression of but narrow national self-interests producing an irrational story, and dismal prospects; even if humanitarian values have continued throughout history at least as a presence (so a potential) for the human condition. Rationality infused with humanistic values can be called upon in the service of human truths.

A significant issue with promoting the activity of reason is that traditional Western interpretations have overwhelmingly tended to prioritise a form of rationalism that is 'logo-centric'. In philosophy this has allowed description and analysis to assume a certain type of expression that involves the translation of the spoken word into mostly restricted written forms and these with an underlying trope of progression from questions/claims, to facts and, via analysis, to resolution/conclusion. A form of rationalizing that can ignore the meaning-rich power of non-Western (non-logo-centric) language forms. This can be dramatically illustrated in Benjamin Lee Whorf's description of the Hopi Indian language, as being comparable to English as the 'rapier to a bludgeon' – a radically different way to describe (and so constitute) Reality; especially in relation to metaphysics; so opening access to finely drawn imaginative ideas. A number of recent post-modern continental philosophers, notably Jacques Derrida, have drawn attention to this prioritising of log-centrism in traditional Western philosophy, if without suggesting a convincing alternative.

Which only realistically leaves us into seeing at least some potential value in taking an openly rational approach to understanding conflictual issues, whilst retaining a preparedness to reformulate the conditions of the rational as a result of experience or of insights drawn from non-logo-centric sources. Rational processes that involve: clarity of definitions, a coherent form of setting out arguments or views, consistency in ideas, and a willingness to consider criticisms within a more general recursive process of authorial self-examination This last can relate to non-logo-centric considerations, and is potentially a key source of redefining the rational process itself if, that is, this process is designed to ever more effectively access Reality and translate its implications into knowledge. Even with his illuminating qualifications, I don't think that Derrida would deny at least some residue of genuine interpretive value in the application of some aspects of rationalism – providing we accept the limitations.

Our enculturalization enwraps us in forms of language regularizing a particular grammatical structure, appropriate phonemic forms, and the use of certain metaphors and analogies, all within an assumed usage. It is difficult to examine the constitution of the wrappings of our 'natural' language if we only have that language itself with which to do so. And yet, critical analysis informed by an understanding of the potential constraints of our language, and perhaps a genuine openness to other language forms, can stimulate our imagination and widen our conceptual horizons even to the point of exposing the '.....vertiginous prospects henceforth opened up for inventive reading.' As noted by Christopher Norris in his 1987 book.

Confidence in the conclusions of any analysis can only ever stand on the foundations of 'faith', but a faith underpinned by a trust in the soundness and intellectual integrity of one's procedures (integrity of the associated reasoning), rather than the type of faith which underpins the dogmatic certainty of all religionists and most ideologues. Meaning inheres within our organicity, even if human cognitive ability provides the means to form a type of awareness we would term 'understanding'; an outcome of a conceived semantic unity allowing us to make sense of our experience.

It seems that social/cultural evolution has provided us as a species with the ability to overcome such threats as are faced by other species, we can use technology to insulate us, at least to some considerable extent, from biological and other dangers. Whether it's that of predatory animals, species threatening disease, or threats to food supplies. But longer-term evolutionary prospects for any species are limited - A species can continue a process of adaptive change, developing in ways (mutational and/or behavioural) conducive to new species formation e.g. some form of earlier Homo (most probably H.erectus) to Homo sapien circa 150,000 y.b.p. - Can become 'fixed' and remain stable as a species for 100s of millions of years e.g. alligator, tortoise, dragonfly - Can find itself in a habitat that, due to dramatic change in environmental conditions, it is unable to adapt to and so becomes extinct e.g. the large-bodied dinosaurs circa 65 m.y.b.p. (following a period of ascendancy lasting for over 160 million years). And even some species of Homo who have left but a fossil record of their existence e.g. Homo neanderthal and Homo denisovan – If they also gifted some droplets of genetic inheritance to Homo sapien.

One of three possible futures awaits our species:

- Continue to evolve on the developing information processing model to become a new species. Just as the species Homo sapien had evolved from a species of Homo erectus some 150,000 years ago. So to evolve from the information processing mode of 'self-consciousness' into the mode that I have termed 'world consciousness?'
- At some point A.I. develops to the level that it then displaces human-beings.
- That Homo sapien becomes extinct (as have millions of species in the past – the headline grouping being the

dinosaurs). This due to making the world unfit for human life......thermonuclear warfare or otherwise dramatic environmental degradation are the two more obvious possible causes.

One of these possible futures will be the fate of our species. I think that the choice is between the first (species change) and the last (extinction). But unlike any other species that has taken one of these two evolutionary paths the introduction of socio/cultural factors, with the corresponding ability to control or destroy, means that the path taken by humankind lies to a considerable extent, in our own hands.

Self-consciousness in Homo sapien is realised in an awareness of itself as a be-ing within a relationship to what is experienced as an external environment separate from itself. Possessing an accessible memory and able to imagine and plan possible futures, with a symbol system (realized in images, expressed emotions, and in language in its widest sense) allowing the re-presentation of information which has led to highly complex scientific and technological advances, to cities, space-craft, the media, mechanised food production, medical-related technological developments, and the means of techno-warfare including nuclear, biological, and chemical weapons, all the lethal so-called conventional weaponry, as well as imaginative philosophical speculation encompassing both formal philosophies and more traditional sources of wisdom. These developments illustrate the presence of contradictory forces within the self-conscious psyche. Past experience can make one pessimistic about which of the two 'choices' already noted will be made by the human species.

But a close consideration of how evolution operates, the way that socio/cultural factors have greatly accelerated this process, and a little imaginative optimism, allows the possibility of a more positive future being open to our species. Self-consciousness in humans can be distinguished from the self-awareness exhibited by other advanced primates in the capacity we have for 'reflection', the extent that we can hold ideas before the mind and follow-up the implications of these – an ability dependent on a memory capacity and projective imagination significantly beyond those of any other primate species.

In terms of the central consideration of this essay, the question of evil primarily as expressed in warfare, it is disagreement at the group (tribe, religion, ethnicity, nation,) levels that in a nuclear-armed world elevates the crucial experiential fault-line in the human condition onto another, a species-critical, level. A fault-line whose sources can be revealed by an examination of the intentional substrate underlying differential perspective-taking for each circumscribed issue where evil is expressed. With this fracture being elevated to species-critical due to two issues confronting humanity: Global issues: - Increasingly unsustainable environmental conditions - Threatened or actual armed conflict (even to the point of thermonuclear war), both between nations and within nations as civil wars. War set off initially by competition over valued resources such as: water, land, fossil fuels, rare and valued metals and minerals, power, and knowledge.

What is required if we are to design global institutional structures that will reconstruct the world in the form of a 'home' for humanity rather than various terrains of contestation in which the powerful relentlessly emerge victorious and the poor and defenceless relentlessly suffer:

- The innovative skills of natural and social scientists......tasked with a purpose.
- The analytic skills of philosophers.......tasked with a purpose.
- The wisdom of leaders unfettered by personal ambition...... tasked with outlining a purpose focused on the Global issues noted above, and of designing institutions of governance suitable for addressing these.
- And of critical importance, the actual engagement of mass populations as a necessary pre-condition to stimulate and sustain the requirements just noted.

The challenge for any individual setting out to confront evil today being the disjunction between action at the personal and local levels, and action at the national and global levels. We can at least attempt to resolve this challenge by, as individuals, reflecting and then deciding upon a realistic action-based balance in our lives, but a balance rooted in authenticity, and emerging from a morality based upon world-conscious values. Michel Foucault, commenting on the responsibility and possibility of authentic self-hood in his 'Politics of Truth' (1997 ed, p158), recommend the night-time practice followed by Seneca ('De Ira') who writes of conducting: '.....an inquest on one's day? What sleep better than that which follows this review of one's action. How calm it is, deep and free, when the soul has received its portion of praise and blame, and has submitted itself to its own examination, its own censure. Secretly, it makes the trial of its own conduct. I exercise this authority over myself as witness before myself........I hide nothing from myself; I spare myself nothing.'

A daily opportunity for the more reflexive consideration of one's life - not some introverted religious contemplation clinging to a self-seeking relationship to a god - not some calculating daily audit on progress towards the achievement of personal material ambitions - but instead, a proactive time located at the end of each day, a time when quietude, and a mode of intense solitary contemplation offers an opportunity for personal life to be considered; the potentially creative opportunity to form an individual's decided ethical stance towards life and lived truth, in which coheres tomorrow's possibilities. It is within this intimate process of personal reflection and decision-making that the resources for authenticity inhere. But it does require some thought-through sense of an appropriate life – of values against which aspirations and behaviour are to be judged. From where does this set of values arise? Foucault (ibid, p156) writes of an: 'hermeneutics of the self', with reference to the ancient Greek Delphic injunction to 'know thyself', set in the wider context of historical processes when at a later time medieval institutions of Christianity and Islam offered an unsatisfactory change in the methodology of self-examination by promoting faith over personal responsibility for others. But I think we could also view this expression ('hermeneutics of the self') as indicating an interpretative boundary between how we do live and how we might formulate the ways in which we should live – reimagining the possible from the actual. The claim that the 'unexamined life isn't worth living' is, in itself a value judgment – the question 'why' stands out. But if we are prepared to rigorously consider the implications of following such an injunction to progress a reflective process of considering the conditions of our lives it becomes a more substantial statement; indeed, it offers a direct challenge to our sense of personal autonomy. Any exercise in progressive revelation should not be just some introspective indulgence seeking to peel off layers of personality to expose some 'real' kernel of personhood that the detritus of everyday concerns and distractions have overlain. Of discovering some deep-seated self that has long been present but only in the form of a nascent presence. Rather, the exercise is more about accomplishment in the sense of being a self-creative revealing of what you might become.

Whilst I would concede that religion continues to play an important support role in the lives of many individuals, the decision to live with the ethical implications of a world conscious level of awareness must be a very personal one - each of us prepared to stand fully exposed to the corscourating blast of lived reality – combining together in action, but to do so as autonomous moral agents fostering the changes, incremental and revolutionary, that can contribute to the construction of a fairer, less evil, world. The emotional and cognitive resources – religious or secular - that we each draw upon matters less than accepting that the outcome is our own responsibility. Indeed doing so sets the parameters within which our authenticity can be defined. It is the originating, personally interpretive, aspect of our experience that offers hope for change. This capacity for creative agency (allied to an aspirational human imagination) offers the basic psychological conditions for the construction of social, economic, and political systems that can provide some humanity-affirming structures, and so is our hope for humanity.

Given the serious and sombre threats of thermonuclear destruction, environmental disaster, domination by A.I., and extreme asymmetries of wealth and power, facing the word today, people whose lives are not constrained by the immediacies of poverty and whose primary concern is not in endeavouring to eke out a living on a daily basis, have a responsibility to determine revolutionary change......but then how can building a world freed from the threat of species catastrophe, and a world in which economic fairness pertains, be revolutionary? Isn't it more about necessary rather than revolutionary change? How do we as individuals deal with the global problems that seem to be beyond any of us in a world whose civil institutions have been constructed by historical circumstances in the interests of the powerful? A world now controlled by national and transnational elites.

Each one of us needs the 'courage to be'. Not in the sense of the media-debased currency of overinflated heroism, but rather to garner the courage that would allow us to realize the potential to be fully human in our lives - to carry a sense of world-consciousness and an awareness of how this more transcendental perspective relates to our daily lives. The courage to stand against injustice, against economic exploitation and social discrimination; against the everyday evils we might chose to pass by being suffered by those that it is convenient to not see - where we rationalize our reluctance to engage. For us to more comfortably adopt the vernacular of humanistic values, and to establish frameworks of solidarity that encompass the dispossessed, the socially repressed, and the economically exploited. The courage to take responsibility for lives lived as workers, as consumers, as neighbours, as friends, and as citizens of the more powerful civil societies. Aspiring to world consciousness would enable each of us to transcend self-consciousness - to connect with the evolutionary potential inherent, if only for now as a latent possibility, in our species.

A difficulty in realizing the constitutive element of courage is to feel that we can be effective - in a world whose institutions are constructed to make us feel discouraged, politically neutered, distracted by entertainment and other forms of wants-based consumerism, and so to be obediently managed. We need to establish and support forums where we can share concerns, reinforce current and create new connections, and build a global sense of common purpose and these at the local, regional, national, and transnational levels. To build a mutually supportive conspiracy of liberation against the forces of control that we must stand against.

A conspiracy initially fostered in our own hearts but one forming and using local, national, and international, connective links, not least those made possible by the internet, to promote and sustain global action. We, each of us, seeking to eschew the everyday accommodations and compromises we might make with obvious injustice. As individuals, we can either obediently align our lives with pathways that just unquestionably accept the normalized relativities of our home society, or we could engage with the world in a significantly different way. To endeavour to use analytic ability and imagination to mentally 'step outside' of the established patterns of our lives - this is the fundamental choice we each have to make. Developing the stance we take to the world following thoroughgoing analysis of central aspects of our lives. It would involve a type of loneliness (or rather 'aloneness') if we do seek to break free of socialized behaviour patterns; especially if these involve an orthodox religious or politically conservative background. But bear in mind that I am not suggesting rejection, the discarding, of what we have come to accept, but rather accepting it on relativised terms and aspiring to transcend this relativity.

Each one of us has at least some tenuous hold on kindness, can be in touch with our humanity. Life-denying, cruel and violent upbringings - the child solider, the bullied or battered child, the baby deprived of adequate nutrition, early exposure to religious fundamentalism or relentless racism - can understandably leave a child or adult deficient in the ability to feel empathy towards others, but for most the potential to do good rather than accept evil is irredeemably present within the depth of our personality. Even those many psychologically wounded, so socially dysfunctional, victims brought up in dehumanizing circumstances might be redeemed with a sufficiency of care, and appropriate support.

We, as individuals, are born within a Reality of which we come to be both confronted with in the sense of having to negotiate our passing through it as well as being within it as a uniquely creative dimension. It confronts and yet includes ourselves; an inextricable relationship gaining a dynamic element from its ever-expanding experiential content.

Immanuel Kant noted his wonder at: 'The starry heavens above me and the moral law within me......I see them before me and connect them immediately with the consciousness of my existence.' This short phrase encapsulates the core aspects of humanity at its best – driven by curiosity to explore the out-there and challenged by our conscience to consider the moral implications of our lives.

This essay has had a primary focus on the evil of conflict and consequently a sense of sadness, and on occasion despair, inevitably runs through it and yet no overview of humankind's collective experience on Earth can entirely miss elements of creativity, joy, kindness, and noble self-sacrifice, that have also been an integral part of this experience, even at times and in places where evil has found expression. In the midst of the darkest of times: in concentration camps, living under the cruellest of dictatorships, during periods of civil and between-nation wars, at the scene of atrocities perpetrated in the name of religion or ethnicity, during bitter industrial strikes, even for the very worst of events individual human beings have sought to mitigate evil and to do good: the street child hidden from pursuers, the crust of bread surreptitiously passed from camp guard to prisoner, the machine gun fired to miss rather than to kill, the bomb aimer silently directing a cluster of bombs towards fields rather than the targeted housing, the South American trades union organizer risking her life to foster solidarity and unite exploited workers, the campesino who organizes his neighbours to stand against the large landowners, the poor man in an African village anonymously paying the school fees of the children of his even poorer neighbour, the bystander living under an oppressive regime who points in this rather than that direction to indicate the passage of the victim fleeing captors....the many, many, witnesses who have stepped forward to become involved when injustice or other evils have been expressed.

Numerous examples noted above (rarely recorded), of the light of human bravery and kindness breaking through the dark veil of evil. The quietude of conscience, the anger at injustice, moving within individuals forced to operate within oppressive political, social, or economic, structures. This represents the golden thread of human kindness that has insinuated itself even at the worst of times, even in the face of the most terrible of evils. This, and in a broader context, the ability to construct social, economic and political systems that can provide some humanity-affirming structures is our hope for humanity.

Nelson Mandela suggested that: 'We have to be taught to hate and if we can be taught to hate then we can be taught to love.' Obvious perhaps, simplistic possibly, but in this short statement Mandela highlights the power of the socialization processes impacting on young people.

Currently most children learn about the world in terms of division, of them and us, of our-kind and their-kind, with a global perspective based on economic competition and political conflict. What might pertain if all the world's children were to learn about intergroup co-operation, economic fairness and social justice, and of peaceful coexistence more generally.

Humanity seems to be capable of so much and yet the same kind of hands that can write a symphony, surgically remove a cancer, carve emotion from a lump of stone, calculate the outcome of a pattern or event observed in a particle accelerator, are also the hands of the same species that have inverted their thumbs to end a defeated combatant's life in the Roman coliseum, wielded an axe to end a life, or fired an automatic rifle to end many more, dashed a baby's head against a rock, held down a women to be raped or a prisoner to be tortured, pressed a button to release a string of bombs, or launched a missile. But behind these actions are human minds; and although the past can foster despair it can also allow hope.

I have noted how we 'find ourselves in existence', doing so in order to express the perspective of a meta-awareness whereby we can view the relativity of our particular situations within a nexus of pre-established relationships and social institutions, and also realising the uniqueness of each of our own experientially formed perspective on life. This perspective can include an awareness of our being present on an ecologically fragile blue/green planet spinning lazily on its axis as it traverses an elliptical passage around the more substantial Sun. These two bodies of the Solar System providing the material means to sustain humankind's journey through time. Echoing Kant ....allowing us to gaze with curious wonder upon the starry skies – and for our imaginations to roam through our lived experience, forming ideas of the possible.

The responsibility we have as individuals, if we commit to foster 'world-consciousness' within ourselves and in our relationships with others, is for us to endeavour to understand the world we find ourselves within and then to seek to move beyond our more local (national, interest-group, religion, tribe, ideology, etc.) interests to ones more likely to improve global conditions for all of its 7.5 billion and rising number of people – both in basic material conditions and for all to be able to experience some 'peace of mind' for their lives and those of their children, grandchildren, and the generations that we hope will follow.

I am suggesting that we have a fundamental moral responsibility to purposefully decide on how we should live, not in term of personal career, close relationships, day to day attitudes, etc (although these would also probably come to be involved) but a deeper level of considering our lives in the context of humanity itself rather than the individual as myself. There is a correspondence between perspective-taking on your own life within Reality in terms of self-creative engagement with a future involving others – the cognitive bridge to world consciousness - and the key task of endeavouring to 'take-up' the perspective of others in relation to this situation or that issue. Each requires us to adopt processes determined to transcend two aspects of our individuality, the first the individual as socialized, the second as an individual prepared to assume a level of social responsibility beyond their more immediate relationships; and each of these as processes of open-ended engagement. Both directed towards transcendence – moving beyond the narrowness of the accidentally socialized and of the self-centring tendencies of self-consciousness.

Life within Being is an ontologically mysterious experience, aspects of the condition being (as noted in the introduction) poetically phrased by Blaize Pascal when he wrote: 'When I consider the short duration of my life, swallowed up in the eternity of before and after, the little space which I fill, and even can see, engulfed in the infinite immensity of spaces of which I am ignorant, and which know me not, I am frightened and am astonished at being here rather than there; for there is no reason why here rather than there, why now rather than then......The eternal silence of these infinite spaces frightens me.' (Taken from Theodosius Dobzhansky, 1976, p.346).

Within this quote we can realize both the insignificance '......swallowed up in the eternity...' but also our uniqueness '.....why here rather than there, why now rather than then....' And it is within this uniqueness that lies not only the responsibility to contribute to humankind's evolutionary potential but also our chance to step forward and live moral lives even in the recognition of life's seeming absurdity. The last being perhaps the hardest most personally autonomous decision – an existential conundrum to be faced or avoided but always there as a brooding presence in our lives. Possibly the boldest action we can each take as an individual is to question ourselves in the world – to create personal authenticity out of deep, open, reflection. Authentic as being self-created in terms of both: our own interior lives to develop a reflexive, if critical, interpretive mode for our experience and also how we become externally directed towards the world.

In order to gain these primary facets of authenticated self-hood you would have worked through the central implications of 'finding oneself within existence'. And this by a consideration of your genealogical connection to the evolutionary, become civil, heritage of our species and of your more immediate connection to the present as a citizen of the world. This is a sombre responsibility, but surely also the most creative grasping of freedom for each of us to Be and so to Become. To Become........entangled with human truth and our human future.

Appendix 1 - Information

I feel that now is the stage of the journey where 'information' has clearly become a key aspect of evolution. Given this, although I have already noted 'information' in the introduction, I now want to consider this key aspect of evolution in a bit more detail. What do I mean by 'information'? Information is that aspect of an environment that is available for an organism, the experiential texture of the 'Reality' within which any organism lives. Information forms a continuum of material and non-material 'substance'.

As the mathematician and cryptographer, Claude Shannon, noted that: 'Nature seems to speak the language of information.'

Organisms process information in order to maintain themselves within an environment. Human-beings (at the top of the hierarchy in relation to information processing capacity) can perceive this 'substance' via the senses and can generate and manipulate more information via their thinking-related activities. Information can be viewed as being a spectrum of complexification ranging from the just noticeable 'difference' in some (external or internal) sensory feature such as temperature, light, appetite, and similar, to the complex nexus of 'difference' that we would encounter with scientific knowledge and more generally the configurations of meaning-infused information that constitutes patterns of our thinking.

The key aspect of information, as it relates to organisms, is 'difference'[6]. Without difference in the stream of internal (bio-psychological) processes and external experience there would be no possibility of awareness. Organisms can only notice differences and this 'notice' could be conscious or unconscious e.g. a molecule in a white blood cell noticing - reacting to - a chemical change such as the presence of a virus in its immediate environment, or a lizard noticing a fly settle nearby, or a human noticing a friend walk into the room. In terms of information content these three examples contain increasing amounts of information being processed.

The manifestation of behaviour informed by the processing of information is a defining characteristic of all life. Depending how deeply (the level of analysis) you wish to analyse what 'processing of information' means for the purpose of my book, it is valid to suggest that inanimate matter does not process information. With such matter as rocks, rivers, iron, and ice, although they do undergo changes

---

[6] Or as 'differeance' noted by the philosopher Jacques Derrida, giving a more conceptual substance in term of the implications of the narrative context of any difference.

('differences') due to changes in environmental conditions i.e. weather, temperature, air pressure, humidity, oxidization, the atmosphere, etc – that do lead to changes in their constitution - this does not involve the processing of information. I accept that inanimate matter does react to environmental conditions in chemical and other physical ways: rocks erode, water precipitates, volcanoes erupt, etc. Vegetable matter (such as trees, plants, fungi, etc) does process information but there is insufficient evidence that such organic life would be 'aware' of doing so, and whether it does so would depend on the definition of awareness. I accept the potential for a detailed philosophical debate on this but for my own more heuristic use of the concept of information processing this is unnecessary.

It becomes more difficult with animal matter (matter that is embodied in organisms). Even the very simplest of micro-organism such as bacteria, and the protista, clearly do process information and I think we can note at least some sense of awareness being present. If that is, 'awareness' is a feature of organisms that can be arranged in terms of a continuum of the considered on its own) marker of information processing capacity, as it relates to evolution, can be the amount of neuronal material available. In species terms we can see that primitive organisms such as sponges and tunicates have no specific neurons (although cells in their bodies can react to environmental conditions - 'differences') but the roundworm (caenorhabditis elegan) has about 300 neurons, the jellyfish 800, sea-slug 18,000, fruit fly 100,000, honey bee 950,000, cockroach 1,000,000, rat 200,000,000, octopus 300,000,000, cat 750,000,000 and human over 86,000,000,000 - so in crude information processing capacity we can see how the species means to access Reality has developed as an adaptive strategy.

Evolution depends upon information processing, without this phenomenon there would not have been any life, and the ways in which organisms process information determines the (species) pattern of evolutionary development. If there is a direction in evolution then I suggest that it should be framed in terms of information processing ability. Let's acknowledge, but leave the issue of computing power for now - currently this issue can quite easily be contained with the standard model of organic evolution. In that we could categorize ICT as but an adjunct to the information-processing capacity of the human species. An aspect of humankind's production of 'cultural' innovation and so similar to: mathematics, writing, books, education, TV/Radio, the internet, each also serving to extend humankinds' own information processing capacity. If, or perhaps rather when, computers meet the necessary criteria for self-reflexion (i.e. awareness - criteria that would also presumably be as applied to humans) with self-replicating software, then I think we will be challenged to re-consider the scope of the current model of evolutionary development - or rather perhaps computer programmes will 'write' this for themselves!

I have so far only referred indirectly to what information is actually constituted by (offering notional clarity as an alternative to precise definition), and I think that this at least to some extent reflects the nature of the phenomenon. Yes, simple sensory stimulation conveys information, aggressive animal behaviours convey information, coloration in animals conveys information, bird-song conveys information, so too does printed, screen-based, and spoken, language, Morse (or any) code, facial gestures, graphic images, mathematical equations, chemical formulas, sets of symbolic logic notation and computer programmes.....etc. etc. all convey information...... but what is it? What are the commonalities, the essential characteristics, by which we can usefully define information? Can we only offer indirect descriptions based on the information content, on the means of its transmission (processing capacity), or on the behaviours that are a reaction to stimuli, or that give rise to the psychological creation of information?

At the level of organic complexity we might suggest that information is the currency of communication[7]; from the simple forms of communication, as in micro-organisms, to its more complex patterns, as in human thinking and interaction with others. If money as currency offers a means of the exchange of goods and services (the memory of stored value), then information as currency is the means of internal and external communication – it makes awareness infused with information possible. And in human 'awareness', allied to a background consciousness, processes structured information constituted by meanings. But, taking a slightly different perspective, we might also describe information as an ('open') medium characterized by difference. Bring these two perspectives together and we can suggest that information is a discontinuous medium that actualizes and sustains behaviours, especially those related to communication and understanding.

It would be fair to suggest that even atoms in the process of forming molecules are sharing information and certainly cellular entities such as mRNA and DNA are involved in responding too and in generating information - throughout its material and conscious

---

[7] There is of course a super-complex range of organic information processing systems - most obviously hormonal, viral, bacteriological, neurotransmission, operating below the level of awareness.

forms life is pervaded with the creation, exchange, and response to, information. A more thorough analysis of evolution in terms of information could offer a useful framework for understanding the underlying generative forces - but definitely not as a quest for any Bergsonian élan vital!

I will leave a more deeply philosophical consideration of the interconnectedness of information, awareness and consciousness, to others better qualified than myself - my own ambitions are narrow and I only wish to use the concept of information as an heuristic tool deployed to better understand 'life', and more especially the evolution of consciousness. Focusing on the implications of information processing, of being involved in 'Reality' (in an evolutionary context) for the human condition.

If I can't offer a direct description of information (some autonomous precise definition decoupled from actually usage) that would satisfy forensic philosophical scrutiny we can at least note one processing mode that is amenable to measurement. Computers are a primary means for conveying the material that constitutes information and a unit used to convey computer-based information is the 'byte'. Each byte is commonly made up of eight 'bits' (there can be less for particular usages) e.g. 11011001 or 01100111, using the two basic digits 0 and 1 generated by electrical pulses in various (practically infinite) configurations of eight bits. In my terminology this would be eight potentials for 'differences' - yes just two digits 0 and 1, so seeming just two differences, but as 11011001 or 01100111 etc. there are eight indicators of difference. We also have differences of the position of each digit, hence a significant potential for 'difference' in the form of a byte.

It is the case that a string of 'bits' (and bytes) can be nonsensical in the sense of not expressing any coherent meanings, but this would not make them 'meaningless' – there remains 'differences' and humans will firstly notice the differences and then seek to project meaning - even if only the meaning of seeming nonsense. Even a secret code is nonsense until decoded. Nonsense is appropriately assigned to any form of information only when its meaning is decided as being nonsensical - to assert that nonsensical strings of letters are meaningless is not the same as stating that it does not convey information beyond simple difference. There is difference so there must be information and so/consequently at least the potential for meaning is always present. The eight basic differences are transcended (in fact sublated would be a more appropriate concept) at the level of the byte (international standard - IEC 80000-13). A byte is used to represent a character such as one letter or one number. At this level of letters and numbers we have a new level of 'difference' to that of the 'bits' 0 and 1. This, number plus letter, innovation increases complexity in that a computer generated letter or number contains the configuration of eight digits then adds something more; as do alphabets, words, sentences, texts, and numerical arrangements. With the 'bit' and the 'byte' as basic units, computer scientists have been able to devise a means of quantifying digital information:

```
an 0 or a 1          = one bit
eight bits           = one byte
one kilobyte(kb)     = 1000 bytes
one megabyte(mb)     = 10002
one gigabyte(gb)     = 10003
one terabyte(tb)     = 10004
one peterabyte(pb)   = 10005
one exabyte(eb)      = 10006
one zettabyte(zb)    = 10007
one yottabyte(yb     = 10008
```

With the yottabyte we have a measure of a massive amount of digital information.

As well having been made amenable to quantification, information also has qualitative aspects, not least the quality of 'meaning' that makes human understanding and communication possible. Language is a structured form for conveying information, a form that allows clarity in our thinking and in our communication with others - it allows the potential conditions for meanings to be purposely, if synthetically, formulated. The production of linguistic expression - internally as well as externally directed communication - is a process where 'vague' thoughts (unformed and perhaps infused with emotions) can progress to take relatively clear linguistic forms - but can also remain as part of the continuous blurred background 'noise'. Infused with pre-linguistic - verging on pre-conscious - emotions, motivations and intentional substrate out of which more formed thoughts can be generated[8]. We are information-processing entities located within information-rich environments. I noted above that information can be viewed in quantitative and qualitative terms; as sense-data the quantitative is more relevant (but not circumscribed by this) and as meaning the qualitative is more relevant (but also not

---

[8] When I write as if thoughts and language 'arise' from a mind I do acknowledge that 'a mind' is inextricably located within a body and a world (psychological, social, and material).

defined by this), for humans and some other species these two are blended together in awareness.

One significant implication of the prioritization of information is that the whole of Reality, all that we can know (possible and actual) - all facts, ideas, emotions, states of affairs, indeed all conceived and conceivable phenomena are constituted by their informational content - 'all' is information. I am suggesting that it would be useful to posit this as a key epistemic (as ontological fact and epistemological limitation) condition for human beings. Reductionist, yes but..........to include a reduction in an analysis would only be problematic if this is the whole procedure rather than only a beginning.

Professor of physics Hans Christian von Bayer suggests a more formal (limited) value for the 'idea' of information, noting that: 'If we can understand the nature of information, and incorporate it into our model of the physical world, we will have taken the first step along the road that leads from the objective reality to our understanding of it' (2004, p17). He distinguishes between a colloquial meaning of information and a technical definition that, although closely intertwined, are profoundly distinct. But he suggests that these two '.....must be reconciled'. He also offers a set of indirect characteristics that can express the nature of information as in: 'In-formation - the infusion of form - the flow of relationships - the communication of messages.' (von Bayer, 2004, p27)

When I use the concept of 'processing' as the way in which organisms engage within information-rich environments, I do not mean to imply 'process' in a linear mode (even if including recursive, feedback-sensitive, regulatory, types of linear processing), similar to the way in which computers process information. If there is a sense in which we can say that organisms are genetically programmed this would just serve as a useful conceptual hook to begin to understand the ways in which organisms are pre-programmed to process information in ways that differ significantly from current types of computer processing. That the genetic programme is subject to considerable and ongoing variation, depending on the outcome of genetic constitution meeting lived experience. The specific details of how human minds (bodies) process information continues as an enigma. But I do think the processing concept, invoking the idea of dealing with information more simply put as 'information in behaviour out', does at least offer a pragmatic means of understanding the behavioural implications of organisms engaging within information-rich internal and external environments.

We are creatures of the creation of informational Reality - not as if 'fish' swimming in a medium of water but rather we are constituted by and constitute the information as a discontinuous medium that just 'is'. The nearest I can get to a philosopher expressing this is Heidegger's concept of Being as Reality, or perhaps just his more personal idea of Dasein's relation to its being, its reality. My capitalization of 'Reality' indicates this as all of the information available in the Universe (so a theoretical idea) – the lower-case 'reality' is that information that is accessible by any individual; so a limitation linked to personal circumstances.

Even just the translation of human biology in terms of computer-type measures of information would reflect the density of the information medium that we are part of. If we consider the human genome: it is constituted by base pairs[9] making up the genetic material in each cell. In the non-sex cell the chromosomes (strings of genes and seemingly non-coding material) take a diploid form i.e. two sets of chromosomes, one from each parent. In 2012 Yevgeniy Grigoryev assumed that each base pair is equivalent to 2 'bit's of information (8 bits to a standard byte) and, using this equivalence, estimated that each human genome stores 1.5 gigabytes of information and that a whole human organism stores 150 zettabytes of information. More recently, George Church and Sri Kosuri (working at Harvard's Wyss Institute) offered a calculation that a single gram of DNA contains 700 terabytes (5.5 Peterabytes) of information. Information is the key medium for understanding the primary functional (and the possibly transcendental as a form of non-deterministic teleology) dynamic of evolution - the medium that can be identified in all forms of life.

So, I posit information as similar to space-time, mass, and energy, as being a fundamental characteristic of the Universe as we know it. In terms of evolution on Earth I suggest that life has evolved in terms of organisms adapting to their environments in ways that exhibit an increasing 'capacity 'to process information – both as simple quantity of information and also in evermore 'novel' forms. In human history this can most clearly be seen by comparing the information-based Reality of circa 10,000 y.b.p and the information-based Reality of the today's twenty-first century. Let's leave consideration of information there for the time being and return to tracking the path of species-evolution as it developed on our planet.

---

[9] A base pair being made of two of: Adenine, Thymine, Cytosine, or Guanine, ATCG - the nitrogenous building blocks of DNA - 3.2 billion bases in the 23 chromosome haploid genome or 6.4 billion bases in 46 chromosome diploid genome.

Appendix 2 - Artificial intelligence – a possible scenario?

Let's consider a possible scenario about 50 years hence: Robotic soldiers, deployed in the field by drone-type guidance systems operated from thousands of miles distance or even self-directed by pre-installed software programmes, are available. Industry, both manufacturing and service, has continued to replace human workers with automated systems. Governments have extended their observation and identification of populations and have the potential to grade individuals according to the extent to which their behaviour aligns with some social 'ideal' (China is already leading in this type of technology). An ideal based on aspects of social acceptability set by governments, or by private industry in line with corporate requirements.

How far could these developments go in but 10, 50, 100 years? Almost all areas of employment will morph from human to machine – just a few being: medical staff, engineers, construction workers, those employed in retail, waste disposal, all forms of transportation, security forces, bankers and those others in financial services, and potentially the most threatening: in the actual manufacture of software and a wide range of robotic machinery. This last including self-replicating A.I. systems, in theory a time when the machines themselves will no longer need humans; noted as 'technological singularity', when technology assumes (and controls) its own momentum and direction.[10]

Globally, millions, probably billions, of humans will have become superfluous to the work-place, few if any current areas of work would be immune to A.I.-related technological change. As nations progress towards overwhelming observation and control of populations and machines have replaced almost all workers how will those in control manage populations? Some of which would invariable become openly disruptive, or in democratic nations would be inclined to use the ballot box to make their concerns known? There are a variety of sophisticated means of persuasion (informed by internet-based analysis of the mass of data harvested from the activities of individuals and groups) that could be deployed to convince the majority of each population group (nation) that in the longer-term the changes will somehow benefit them; no doubt also mobilising the threat of external competition as an additional persuader.

---

[10] It might be that some more culturally colourful 'primitive' groups are allowed to continue to occupy traditional sites so serving as destinations for wealthy tourists.

Another placatory action could be the introduction of a 'social wage' paid to all in order to soften the impact of unemployment and to allow economic demand for goods and services to be maintained. So a wage that would simply be recycled back into the production process, with goods made cheaper by the efficiency of machine and robotic production, and the disposal of the more costly human work-force. With any recalcitrant individuals or leaders of minority groups (perhaps any surviving trade unions or more libertarian or socialist political parties) reluctant to accept this direction of change, being imprisoned or even 'disposed of'; the severity of the means of suppressing dissent will invariably increase as this projected A.I. revolution progresses.

The current advances in communication and control technologies and those that have taken place in global financial control, form the base from which incremental change can continue to shift power towards elite economic and/or political groups. The past 40 years of state subsidised neo-liberal advance has already seen a significant shift in power towards the global financial elites especially when (as in Russia and China) these are in direct control of governments. A.I. and its associated robotics offer the potential to vastly increase the power of those who control its development and deployment. Currently, control is relentlessly moving towards global elites, democratic regimes have done little to mitigate this and dictatorial regimes have actively encouraged it.

When the technology has advanced to a time when control can be exercised in a way perceived to be fully in the interest of elites then the question would arise – leaders of elites might ask - why do we need potentially disruptive populations that are not 'of us', or are in the relatively small servant-class that we might still need to maintain our luxurious lives? If A.I. based machines can produce the food, construct the buildings, run transport, care for health and attend to all personal needs (even virtual, or otherwise mechanized, sex might become a favoured option – and there would always be the surviving servant class to draw on for this pleasure) why do the controlling elites need the billions who would then do nothing for them, their potential for productive labour being superfluous.

But the masses do contribute massively to polluting the environment, a clear threat even for the super-rich. So there would be a rationale to begin a process of eliminating all but say 100 -200 million individuals making up the global elites and their necessary human support systems. Allowing an over 7 billion reduction in the population of the world – a powerful, if seriously inhuman, means of dramatically reducing global warming, resource depletion, and pollution!

Who would be able to prevent this elimination gained by global 'holocaust', or gained by just removing all but basic healthcare provision and introducing a no-child policy for the masses? Any resistance at this time could be ruthlessly put down by robotic security forces unburdened by any moral inhibitions. Even if these cyber-troopers are still controlled by some surviving human military (who would themselves be members of elites), I am sure most generals would value being able to deploy these 'ideal' military units: highly efficient killing capability, totally amoral and completely obedient. If there were any 'casualties' these would not be deaths but merely repairable breakdowns in machines, so no bereaved parents to write too, no demoralization of fellow soldiers, no PTSD, only a redirection to some repair facility, one no doubt run by robots!

Is this merely some science fiction dystopia or is it a possible scenario whose catastrophically evil outcome will have been attained by stealth, as power and control is incrementally shifted even more towards global elites and the A.I. based means to enforce obedience has been developed. The numerous gated and high-security patrolled communities enabling the wealthy only having to mix with the wealthy, are already being constructed (and increasing in number at an exponential rate), the 40 year shift in global economic power toward rentier elites, the increase in what are effectively political dictatorships and the mainly uncontrolled frontiers of A.I. development, are early indicators of what could come to pass. The pollution of the planet, the increasing instability with the current capitalist economic system, and the threat these could offer to the current dominant elites, provide the motivational drivers for such change. Who controls our future? Who controls A.I., and how they might do so, could be an appropriate and urgent question for us to address.

Appendix 3 - Global governance and re-imagined United Nations

It would be difficult to 'design' a system of global governance that would not be liable to being misused by some vested interest – be they some elite-group, nation-state, global finance, religion, etc. – For most obvious forms of misuse – corruption, bribery, nepotism, promoting a single group's interest, subversive cyber-infiltration - a system can be made quite robust. But any system of governance can only be successful to the extent that it enjoys public respect and ongoing support.

Re-construction of the UN would require the fundamental agreement of nations to concede sovereignty – certainly over the right to go to war, economic arrangements that involve global finance, and environmental matters, and ideally over a whole range of human rights issues.

I am sure that a combination of jurists, constitutional academics, civil servants, and reflective representative politicians, can design a better Global governance system than myself. One that can best balance the various (at times potentially/seemingly competing) interests and asymmetric power available to those whose lives any reconstructed UN would be responsible for – if any balance would need to prioritise the 'voice' of the world's people as this relates to progressing the founding principles and aims of any UN charter. But I will make a few suggestions on the sort of organization that could bring the world into participatory governance more to frame a debate on this than to offer detailed prescriptive guidance.

Balance of interests and powers:

A primary assembly composed of each nation's leader (rotating if a nation has a leadership groups rather than a single leader) or their direct representatives (no Security Council) – so approx.. 194 delegates – each with one vote.

A second chamber of elected representatives (ideally elected by continents or regions rather than nations) but elected in relation to size of a population. I would assume some bottom-up, tiered system, from elected very local representatives to within-nation regional, to national, to inter-nation regions.

This second UN chamber of 300 elected representatives (each representing about 23m people – fixed term of 5 years). Each supported by a back office of 'civil servants' (from a central 'pool' of trained administrators) providing factual information (focused on the regions represented) sourced primarily from a more central, determinedly independent, UN data-producing and advisory office.

In addition to this more representative structure there would also be some judicial body whose primary task would be to assess and declare a ruling on the interpretation of the UN Charter by the first and second assemblies (chambers). Ideally this judicial body would be composed of 5, 7, or 9, 'wise' individuals with some experience of interpretive law i.e. appeal courts or other types of constitutional experience. I would have thought that appointments for the 'High Court' could be made by the second chamber. If from a shortlist identified by civil servants applying some 'objective' assessment combining judicial experience in itself and to some extent some commitment to the values expressed in the UN Charter that has been reflected in applicant's careers/lives. It might be appropriate that these appointments are relatively short-term 3-5 years. These people need to be motivated by an international perspective that is entirely focused on the UN Charter – In the 'normal' course of UN business the role of this body would be to consider First Chamber decisions in a light touch way, but that, if they consider that a decision would be judged to definitely infringe the Charter they can: either advise that it be reconsidered by both chambers: or following more detailed consideration might rule it 'unconstitutional' and so unable to be implemented; or it be accepted, perhaps with 'advisory' reservations. At all stages this 'high' constitutional/charter court would primarily be seeking to work co-operatively with the two principle chambers.

If a decision of the First Chamber was challenged by at least 10% of the membership of the second chamber this could also be referred to the constitutional court for reconsideration – it would be expected that any such 'appeal' would be made on the basis of some identification of where any First Chamber decision being challenged does not comply with the terms of the UN Charter.

Agencies of the UN:

- Global Peace and Security agency (including responsibility for refugees)
- Global Financial/Economic Committee
- Global Environment agency
- Global Health agency
- Global Education agency
- Global Governance committee
- Global Science and Technology agency
- Global Data Coordinating agency

The work of current UN agencies – Maritime, Aviation, Meteorology, Food and Agriculture, Labour, Atomic energy and Weaponry, Tele- and Postal communications, Intellectual property rights, cultural issues, etc. – to be incorporated within the new Global agencies noted above.

I would also suggest a UN public news and information service undertaking in-depth news analysis and even-handed presenting of 'factual' news presented in relevant contexts. I accept this might be contentious..... who judges 'relevant contexts' – I think that the credibility of such an organization will at least be judged against current broadcasters, the quality of almost all of whom it would not be difficult to improve on in terms of both 'factual objectivity' and 'relevant context'.

The work being undertaken by each of the agencies being directly overseen by a small body composed of either only representatives drawn from of the Second Chamber or some balance of these and senior global civil servants.

(The operational approach of the UN's current UNICEF/ UNESCO/WHO could perhaps serve as a model for some of the agencies)

Remuneration of representatives:

First Chamber: As these would be representatives of national governments it would be appropriate that home governments determine the pay and conditions of these.

Second Chamber: Each representative's pay should be based on the average income of families of the 23m people they represent, plus 50% to recognise responsibility. All expenses directly applying to their UN work (private office support, travel, accommodation, other living costs, etc) should be paid from a central UN fund.

Global High Court: Judges for this body should be paid the average pay of all the Second Chamber representatives, plus 50% to recognise responsibility. These suggested levels of financial remuneration might seem quite modest by today's standard but bear in mind the social status of these positions and the central role they would have in global governance meaning that they should set an example of modest material ambitions. There would also need to be some independent body that monitors expense claims and the potential for bribery and corruption – not least to show the represented population that such measures were in place.

The role, if any, for lobby groups would also need some detailed consideration – In terms of relevant information on an issue, the sort of special perspective any company, interest group, sectional interest, and similar could of course be relevant to inform decision-making. But I feel these should be more as ad hoc representative delegations meeting up with sub-committee members from the First or Second Chambers, or even able to address all members of each assembly if an issue is considered as being of particular important.

Funding for the UN (possibly separate from the Global Finance Committee (GFC) noted Dyer 2021) should come from governments, primarily in line with some formula based on per capita income of each country as a key element.

PROPOSALS FOR THE ESTABLISHMENT OF A GENERAL INTERNATIONAL ORGANIZATION [1]

There should be established an international organization under the title of The United Nations, the Charter of which should contain provisions necessary to give effect to the proposals which follow.

CHAPTER I. PURPOSES

The purposes of the Organization should be:

1. To maintain international peace and security; and to that end to take effective collective measures for the prevention and removal of threats to the peace and the suppression of acts of aggression or other breaches of the peace, and to bring about by peaceful means adjustment or settlement of international disputes which may lead to a breach of the peace;
2. To develop friendly relations among nations and to take other appropriate measures to strengthen universal peace;
3. To achieve international cooperation in the solution of international economic, social and other humanitarian problems; and
4. To afford a centre for harmonizing the actions of nations in the achievement of these common ends.

CHAPTER II. PRINCIPLES

In pursuit of the purposes mentioned in Chapter I the Organization and its members should act in accordance with the following principles:

1. The Organization is based on the principle of the sovereign equality of all peace-loving states.
2. All members of the Organization undertake, in order to ensure to all of them the rights and benefits resulting from membership in the Organization, to fulfil the obligations assumed by them in accordance with the Charter.
3. All members of the Organization shall settle their disputes by peaceful means in such a manner that international peace and security are not endangered.
4. All members of the Organization shall refrain in their international relations from the threat or use of force in any manner inconsistent with the purposes of the Organization.
5. All members of the Organization shall give every assistance to the Organization in any action undertaken by it in accordance with the provisions of the Charter.
6. All members of the Organization shall refrain from giving assistance to any state against which preventive or enforcement action is being undertaken by the Organization.

The Organization should ensure that states not members of the Organization act in accordance with these principles so far as may be necessary for the maintenance of international peace and security.

CHAPTER III. MEMBERSHIP

1. Membership of the Organization should be open to all peace-loving states